The title says it all...

More heart problems result directly from poor food selection, and consequent poor metabolism of essential nutrients, than any other cause. Yet, more often than not, we end up making wrong choices. Sometimes out of ignorance, and sometimes under the mistaken belief that healthy food is not delicious.

Eat Sensible, Eat Balanced.

Eat fresh, simple foods and your body will make good use of them. More processing means more problems. Don't try to avoid cholesterol containing foods – you can't, if you hope to maintain good nutritional balance. Instead eat foods that will provide ammunition against cholesterol accumulation and protect your heart.

Live Healthy, Look Great.

This book brings you all the information you need about healthy eating. The author provides comprehensive information on nutrition, calorie, fat and cholesterol contents of various foods, and a round-up of foods and recipes that will extend the life of your heart.

Authoritative. You may not want to live forever, but you would certainly like to be healthy for as long as you possibily can. This book will help you do so.

The Author

G. Padma Vijay is a trained nutritionist with deep interest and research experience in clinical nutrition (on obesity). She holds multiple postgraduate diplomas in Nutrition, Diatetics and Psychological Counselling and has worked as a researcher in Clinical Nutrition at SNDT Women's University, Mumbai and taught at Modern College, Mumbai. She earned her Masters degree in Plant Science from Osmania University after graduating in Chemistry and Biology.

Her articles on health and nutrition appear regularly in several magazines and newspapers; including *Femina* and *The Times of India*. She lives in Mumbai and runs a Diet Therapy and Nutrition Clinic there.

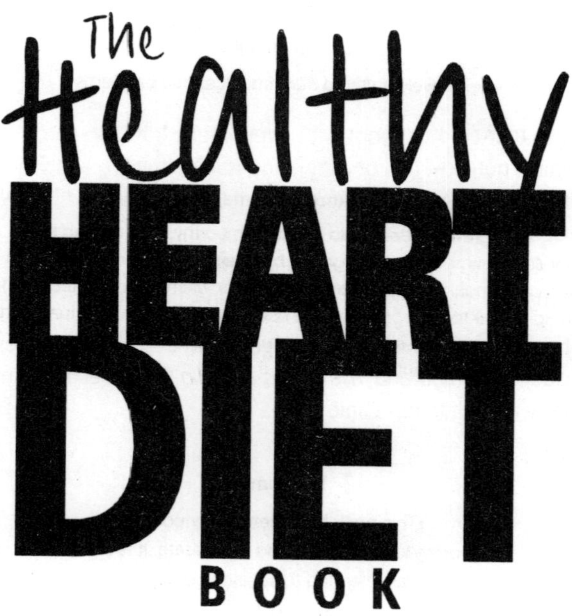

G Padma Vijay

Dedicated to my Late Father
D. Ramamurthy
who bravely suffered numerous cardiac problems.

Acknowledgements

I am greatly indebted to Dr. Ramamoorthy, who spared his valuable time to go through the book and write a Foreword. I am extremely thankful to Dr. Mohan Chitnis for writing the Preface and for helping me to incorporate some useful information about the heart. Above all, my sincere gratitude to my husband Vijay, who has constantly encouraged me in all my endeavours.

Disclaimer

This book has been designed to provide information and to educate. It is in no way intended to substitute or replace medical counselling.

www.orientpaperbacks.com

ISBN : 978-81-222-0344-8

1st Published 2003
6th Printing 2015

Healthy Heart Diet Book

Cover design by Vision Studio

Published by
Orient Paperbacks
(A division of Vision Books Pvt. Ltd.)
5A/8 Ansari Road, New Delhi-110 002

Printed in India at
Saurabh Printers Pvt. Ltd., Noida

Cover Printed at
Ravindra Printing Press, Delhi-110 006

Foreword

There is no doubt in my mind that many diseases can be managed by a commonsense attitude towards diet and physical exercises, and with minimum of medication. The increase in the incidence of Ischaemic heart disease throughout the world can be ascribed to many factors – among them dietary indiscretion and lack of exercise being self-inflicted causes.

Ms. Padma Vijay has written this book keeping in mind the critical importance of diet management in the treatment of, and recovery from, heart diseases. Apart from the details regarding the preparation of healthy, nutritive and low cholesterol foods, the book includes the nutritive value of each recipe. To make it simpler and practical the corresponding Indian names of foods have been listed in the glossary.

I am sure that this well-written book will find wide acceptance not only with patients suffering from heart disease, but also with healthy individuals, who will find a lot of information in controlling and preventing heart diseases and obesity.

I wish the book all success.

Dr. K. Ramamoorthy

Founder Fellow, Indian College of Physicians
Hon. Physician & Hon. Prof. of Medicine
Bombay Hospital Institute of Post Graduate Medical Sciences

Introduction

High levels of stress have become a hallmark of living and working in the present times. Life, both domestic and professional, has become faster and more demanding. As a result, stress related health problems such as hypertension, cardiac problems, diabetes, ulcers, insomnia and headache are on the increase.

The heart is really the heart of the human body. Its smooth, trouble-free functioning depends on the proper use or misuse of our bodies. Unfortunately, the patterns of modern living and the increasing reliance on technology have resulted in development of a lackadaisical attitude towards finding time for our health. It is only when we face a heart problem do we realise the damage we may inadvertently have done to our health.

But there is the good news as well. With proper care, diet and physical activity, even those challenged with a heart condition can lead a normal, healthy life and not be denied the pleasure of good food. That is the purpose of this book.

Foods can, and do, heal the heart. The variety of food choices, traditional and contemporary – a virtual food fiesta – available in our part of the world is amazing. With a slight modification in the cooking methods or in the ingredients, most food becomes healthier and good for the heart, improving the quality of life and adding to longevity.

I have endeavoured to provide low-calorie, low-cholesterol, recipes that do so, without affecting the flavour, taste or the pleasures of a good meal.

G. Padma Vijay

Mumbai, April, 2003

Preface

While there is no dearth of media attention being given to diet, there has been little focussed effort to provide authoritative information on nutrition and diet for a healthy heart. The scanty advice given by the busy doctor is seldom fully understood. The family members who have the critical task of providing healthy and healing diet to heart patients often rely on incomplete information or on hearsay. They now have a choice.

I am glad that G. Padma Vijay has written a complete book that attempts to answer all the questions that a heart patient or his family members may have about healthy and unhealthy foods. More important, she explains why some foods are better than others for the health of the heart. The language is simple and easy-to-understand. The advise is practical and easy-to-follow in day-to-day life. It is based on solid scientific principles and backed by medical studies.

The coverage is comprehensive. All aspects of a healthy heart diet have been discussed – calorie intake, salt consumption, the role of fats and oils, the planning of menus and much more.

Acknowledging that food occupies an important place in life, more than 130 low calorie, low fat and cholesterol free recipes have been given in the book.

I have no hesitation in recommending this book and congratulating the author on completing a much needed job.

Dr. Mohan Chitnis

Sadguru Hospital, New Bombay

Contents

Understanding Your Heart

CHAPTER I

The Heart how it works

The heart is a strong, efficient muscular pump which drives blood through a network of blood vessels – arteries, veins and capillaries – to every part of the body. No part of the body can function properly and efficiently without a constant and adequate supply of blood.

The heart is about the size of a clenched fist. It is located slightly to the left of the centre of the chest. Breastbone protects it from the front, the spinal column from the back and the lungs from either side. It has three layers of tissue: the myocardium, the epicardium and the endocardium.

The muscle responsible for pumping the blood is called myocardium. It is the thick main layer of heart muscle. Outside surface of heart is covered by a thin, glossy membrane called the epicardium. Another smooth, glossy membrane, which covers the inside surfaces of the heart's four chambers, the valves, and the muscles attached to valves is called endocardium.

There is also a protective membrane known as the pericardium which encloses the entire heart in a sac.

Structure of the Heart

The heart is divided into four chambers. The two upper chambers are called atria – the left atrium and the right atrium. They act as receiving chambers for the blood from the lungs and the body.

The two lower chambers are called ventricles – the left and right ventricles. They are the pumping chambers. They pump the blood out to the lungs and to all parts of the body through the arteries.

The Heart: An Efficient Double Pump

The heart functions as two adjacent pumps, the right half and the left half, with each half having a receiving room (atrium) on the top, and a pumping room (ventricle) at the bottom.

The right half pumps the blood to the lungs via pulmonary circulation system where it is oxygenated. The oxygen-rich, refreshed blood travels from the lungs to the left half or left side of the heart.

On receiving the oxygen rich blood from the lungs, the left half pumps the refreshed blood to all parts of the body where it gives oxygen to the cells and picks up carbon dioxide, a waste product, and brings it to the heart. The blood returning back from the body is received in the right half and pumped out to the lungs for fresh supply of oxygen.

The amount of blood that enters and leaves the two left-half chambers is exactly the same as that passes through the right-half of the heart.

The heart works or pumps in cycles. During the first phase of each cycle the atria (the upper chambers) contract and the blood is pushed into the ventricles (the lower and much larger chambers). In the second phase the filled up ventricles contract and push the blood out into the lungs and to the rest of the body, while the atria fill up.

The Rhythm of Your Heart : A healthy heart beats steadily and rhythmically at a rate of 60 to 90 beats per minute, pumping out about 4.5 to 5 litres of blood every minute. To accomplish this pumping, the heart spontaneously and repetitively generates electric impulses, which organise and trigger the sequence of heart muscle contractions during each heart beat. The pattern and timing of the sequence determines the rhythm. A heart beat is the action of blood being pumped out of the heart.

The heart rate increases when a person becomes excited or frightened, during an illness or while exercising. This is the body's natural response to stress. In its strenuous daily routine, the heart pauses to rest for a split second between beats.

Understanding Blood Pressure: Blood pressure is the force, or the pressure, of the blood against the walls of the blood vessels – the arteries and the veins – in the body. It is needed to maintain the blood supply to all organs and structures of the body. Without this pressure, the blood would not be able to circulate in the body.

The pumping action of the heart has two phases – first, when it contracts and forces the blood out into the body and the lungs, and second, when the heart expands (or relaxes) and fills up with blood. This two stage action translates into two different pressures exerted by the blood on the walls of the blood vessels. These are called systolic pressure and diastolic pressure.

- Systolic pressure is pressure at the moment when the heart contracts and pumps the blood out. It represents the moment of greatest pressure of the blood against the walls of the arteries and veins.
- Diastolic pressure is the pressure when the heart expands (or relaxes) and fills up. This represents the moment of the least pressure of the blood against the walls of the arteries and veins.
- The systolic pressure is always higher than the diastolic pressure.

Blood pressure is measured in units of millimeters of mercury (mm Hg), which corresponds to the height of the column of mercury in the sphygmomanometer–the instrument doctors use for taking blood pressure. A normal blood pressure reading for an adult is in the range of 120 (systolic)/80 (diastolic) to 139/89 mm Hg (systolic/diastolic). (See page 45).

The Circulatory System: Your Arteries and Veins

The heart receives blood through the veins, pumps it to the lungs, receives it from the lungs and distributes it through the arteries to all parts of the body.

The major arteries that carry blood from the heart are the aorta and the pulmonary arteries. The coronary arteries which supply the heart muscle with blood branch off directly from the aorta.

Veins return blood to the heart. The large veins that enter the heart are the superior vena cava (from head or arms), the inferior vena cava (from abdomen or legs) and the pulmonary veins.

This circulation is achieved through three different sub-circulation systems. The three types of circulation are:

Systemic Circulation: The circulation of the blood through the aorta and its branches to organs, tissues and cells of the body and its return into the heart is known as the systemic circulation.

Coronary Circulation: The muscles of the heart are fed by the right and the left coronary arteries. The deoxygenated blood from the muscles of the heart returns to the right atrium through a network of veins and this constitutes the coronary circulation.

Pulmonary Circulation: The circulation of blood from the right ventricle of the heart to the lungs for oxygenation and its return into the heart constitutes the pulmonary circulation.

The circulatory system also helps in forming clots to mend injured areas, regulates the body temperature and fluid balance. Any abnormalities in the heart's structure and function leads to various diseases and disorders.

CHAPTER 2

Understanding Heart Disease Causes and Symptoms

Heart diseases affect people of all ages, but the middle-aged are more affected. In the early stages, heart diseases do not manifest any symptoms; in fact, heart diseases give rise to a relatively limited range of symptoms. Only in the later stages are the more obvious symptoms such as chest pain, pain in the arm, weakness, fatigue, palpitations and shortness of breath seen.

The management of cardiovascular ailments requires rest, investigating the causes followed by treatment through a combination of drugs, surgery, and through modification of diet. In all cases, except congenital heart diseases or those due to genetic factors, it is possible to reduce the risk of heart disease by a change in lifestyle. Congenital heart diseases, which are diseases that occur at birth, such as valve disease, or diseases due to infections, do not have relation to diet or lifestyle. However, diet is important in strengthening the body's immunity against infections.

Diseases of the Heart Muscle

Diseases affecting the heart muscle are known às cardiomyopathies. These lead to gradual loss of the efficiency of the heart to act as a pump.

Causes: These include fibrosis (growth of dense fibrous tissue) of the endocardium — the inner layer of the heart wall — and the myocardium, valvular defects, heart muscle disease, alcoholic heart disease, coronary heart disease, enlargement of the ventricles and changes in the structure and number of chromosomes caused by free radicals.

Symptoms: The symptoms of cardiomyopathies are a jerky pulse, arrhythmia or abnormal heart rhythms, angina or chest pain, breathlessness, enlargement of the ventricles and the atria, heart failure, occasional loss of consciousness and sometimes sudden death.

Treatment: Treating the underlying disorder with medication and a change in lifestyle can prevent further complications like heart failure. The best prevention is a healthy lifestyle.

Ischaemia or Coronary Heart Disease

This is the commonest form of heart disease and the single most important cause of premature death in the developed world. Ischaemia or coronary heart disease occurs when the coronary arteries get blocked due to the build up of deposits, known as plaque, on their inner walls. This prevents sufficient supply of blood from reaching the myocardium.

Causes: The main cause of coronary heart diseases is atherosclerosis, which is the hardening of the arteries due to deposits of plaque and thrombosis, or blood clots.

The risk of coronary heart disease increases with age. Men are more prone to coronary heart disease. However, postmenopausal women are at equal risk. This disease often runs in families, and persons with family history of heart disease are at high risk.

Individuals who smoke, drink, have diabetes, high blood pressure, increased cholesterol and triglyceride levels, and increased fibrinogen (a protein that helps in the clotting of blood) are more prone to coronary artery disease. So are the obese, physically inactive, stressed and those who have diets rich in saturated fats and low in antioxidants. People with a combination of risk factors such as smoking, hypertension and diabetes, have a greater chance of developing coronary heart disease than those with only one risk factor.

Symptoms: The usual symptom is severe chest pain which may radiate to the neck, jaw and upper or even lower arms.

Treatment: Investigations to diagnose the underlying cause are necessary. Management of the disease is by rest, medication and modified diet.

Prevention: To reduce the risk of developing coronary heart disease, it is best to discontinue smoking and drinking and to maintain ideal body weight through regular exercise. Learning to cope with stress and eating a low fat diet go a long way in helping to prevent coronary heart disease.

Atherosclerosis: Narrowing of the Arteries

Narrowing of the arteries due to accumulation of fatty deposits, cholesterol and other materials on the inner lining is called atherosclerosis. This gradual buildup of plaque narrows the cavity or the channel through which the blood flows, reduces the circulation and increases risk of heart attack and stroke, specially among the elderly. Though atherosclerosis usually affects the coronary arteries, other arteries can also be affected.

Causes: The primary cause of atherosclerosis is high blood cholesterol levels due to increased total fat in the diet. Other factors such as high blood pressure, cigarette smoking and diabetes also promote development of plaque. (See page 35).

Symptoms: Since the process of accumulation of fatty streaks and the consequent loss of pliability and flexibility of arteries starts in adolescence and is often well advanced by middle age, few or no symptoms are seen.

Treatment: The management of atherosclerosis is through medication and modified diet. Strict moderation or giving up alcohol is recommended. Other precautions include giving up smoking, maintaining ideal body weight, maintaining low blood cholesterol levels, exercising regularly and following a modified diet plan.

Risk Factors: Though atherosclerosis usually occurs with ageing, it is also often seen in smokers and people with high cholesterol levels. Men are more at risk than women who are protected in their reproductive years by the hormone estrogen which keeps their cholesterol under control. However, after menopause women are at equal risk. People who are obese, hypertensive, lead sedentary lives, are often stressed and smoke and drink in excess, are also at risk. Even passive smokers run a high risk.

Thrombosis

Clotting is the natural response of body to bleeding and loss of blood from an injury. But when an unusual blood clot called the thrombus, which is primarily made up of sticky platelets, forms inside a blood vessel, it blocks the flow of blood. A coronary artery thus blocked deprives the heart muscle of blood, and can trigger a heart attack. This intravascular clotting is called thrombosis.

Causes: These include atherosclerosis, sluggish blood flow and smoking. Chest pain as a result of mild exertion and breathlessness are the symptoms of thrombosis.

The elderly, persons who smoke and drink in excess, the obese, the physically inactive, those who have high blood pressure and elevated blood lipids (blood fat) are at high risk.

Treatment: Treatment for thrombosis is rest, medication and a modified diet. As in atherosclerosis, moderate consumption of alcohol or abstaining from it, giving up smoking, weight control through regular exercise and a modified diet are the best ways to guard against thrombosis.

Myocardial Infarction (MI) or Heart Attack

The destruction or death of the heart muscle due to failure of blood supply caused by thrombosis is called a heart attack. Medically, it is known as myocardial infarction or coronary thrombosis. If the area of the damaged muscle is not large and the attack has not interfered with the heart's pumping ability, the victim usually recovers and can resume normal activities within two to three weeks. Such patients carry a healing scar on the heart muscle and have an increased risk of a second infarct or may become severely disabled.

If the damaged heart muscle area is large and the oxygen-starved muscle disturbs the rhythmic heart beat, sudden death can occur unless the rhythm is restored immediately with a machine called the defibrillator. If a defibrillator is not available, he or she can be kept alive by heart-lung resuscitation (massage and artificial respiration).

Causes: Coronary artery disease is the main cause of myocardial infarction. The infarction is usually due to formation of a thrombus which then blocks the atherosclerotic coronary artery. Sometimes there is no thrombosis but because of the narrowing of the coronary artery the blood flow is insufficient, and the cardiac muscles are starved of, or get insufficient supply of blood.

Persons who smoke and drink alcohol in excess and have increased serum (blood fat) levels are at high risk, as are people who are obese or have diabetes or hypertension.

Symptoms: Pain is the cardinal symptom of MI. It comes even when a person is at rest. It is very severe and constricting, and lasts for hours. The pain spreads to the throat, arms or back, and is accompanied by general symptoms such as breathlessness, nausea, vomiting, weakness, sweating, low urine output, cold peripheries, and low blood pressure. Pain, however, is not typical in all patients; some patients, like the elderly and the diabetics, may suffer from MI without experiencing pain and other physical signs, while others may look very ill. Some may show stress symptoms, such as anxiety, tension, increased heart beats and the frightening feeling of impending death.

Most symptoms of MI are due to left ventricular dysfunction, pulmonary oedema (swelling in the lungs) and low cardiac output or inadequate pumping of the blood by the heart.

Sudden death due to cardiogenic shock or cardiac arrest may occur within the first hour. If the patient survivies this critical stage, the liability to dangerous arrhythmias – abnormal rhythms of the heart – remains, but diminishes with each passing hour.

Treatment: If the breathing and pulse of a victim of MI are normal, keep him warm and seek professional help immediately. If the breathing has stopped and the pulse is absent, the person may be dead but may sometimes respond to emergency treatment such as heart-lung resuscitation, which essentially involves massaging the heart while giving mouth to mouth artificial respiration.

Early management of MI is bed rest, immediate medical attention, which includes investigations, medication and a change in lifestyle.

Prevention: Those who are overweight or obese should reduce their weight and their total serum cholesterol. Smoking and drinking are not recommended. Hypertension, or high blood pressure, and diabetes should be kept under control. Stress should be dealt with by using relaxation techniques.

Angina Pectoris (Chest Pain)

Angina pectoris is the term used to describe discomfort due to pain in the chest and constitutes a symptom rather than a disease. An angina attack is not a heart attack and there is no damage to the heart muscle.

Angina occurs as a crushing, squeezing pain when the heart muscle does not get enough blood and oxygen supply. Patients may live for many years with this condition as long as they keep within the exercise tolerance limits. However, they carry an increased risk of sudden death or myocardial infarction, especially if they undertake any unusual exertion. Since angina builds up in proportion to the intensity of exertion, it limits the patients' physical activities.

Causes: Coronary arteries become less elastic and increasingly narrow (due to plaque deposits) with age. In other words, angina is the result of atherosclerosis; while the arteries may be wide enough to provide sufficient blood during rest, they are unable to supply enough oxygen-rich blood when physical activity increases the demand on the heart. Any exertion, not only exercise or climbing a staircase, but even excitement or increased emotional stress, can cause angina.

People who smoke, are obese, have diabetes, anaemia, high blood pressure and high blood cholesterol levels are high risk candidates. It is common among the middle aged and the elderly.

Symptoms: Patients experience a squeezing, crushing, burning or aching pain in the chest as well as discomfort. The pain is seldom of the stabbing type. This pain may radiate down either arm, across the chest and up to the neck, even to the jaw or through to the back. The patient sweats and experiences weakness. There is a choking sensation resulting in shortness of breath, palpitations, nausea and a light headache. The pain increases in intensity until it reaches a plateau and then diminishes. An attack can last up to ten to fifteen minutes, or longer. The symptoms worsen after a meal and in a cold weather.

Prevention: Patients should reduce stress and learn to relax. Yoga and meditation can reduce the frequency and the intensity of angina attacks. A relaxed lifestyle, regular, moderate exercise, and weight control are advised. Smoking and being in smoky places is harmful. Exercise after a heavy meal or in very cold weather should be avoided.

Any pain in and around the chest should not be ignored; a physician should be consulted immediately.

Arrhythmias: Abnormal Rhythms and Palpitations

These are disturbances in the electrical activity of the heart. In other words, they are the abnormal rhythms of the heart, causing it to beat irregularly or unusually fast or slow for extended periods. This disrupts the normal circulation of blood. Bradycardia is defined as a rate of heart beat less than 60/min, whereas, tachycardia is the rate of heart beat exceeding 100/min.

Causes: An infection of the heart, coronary artery disease or a heart valve defect can cause arrhythmias. Other causes are thyroid or kidney disease, certain drugs, imbalance of potassium or magnesium in the body, high intake of caffeine rich beverages and alcohol, heavy smoking and stress.

Persons who are already suffering from a heart disease, those who smoke, drink and can't cope with stress are at higher risk.

Symptoms: The symptoms may include chest pain, weakness, fatigue, dizziness, loss of consciousness, palpitations, shortness of breath, light headedness, fluttering in the chest or neck. At other times there are no symptoms and arrhythmias may go unnoticed for a long time unless diagnosed by a physician.

Treatment: This includes medication and rest. Regular exercise, coping with stress, practicing relaxation techniques, moderate intake of alcohol and avoiding caffeinated beverages can prevent arrhythmias.

Congestive Heart Failure (CHF)

In congestive heart failure, a weakened heart is unable to pump as efficiently as it should and not enough oxygen-rich blood reaches all parts of the body. As the blood flow from the heart slows down (low cardiac output), the blood returning to the heart backs up leading to 'congestion' in the tissues. Fluids can accumulate in the lungs and in the ankles. In the mildest forms of heart failure, cardiac output is adequate at rest and becomes inadequate only when the demand increases during physical exertion or other forms of stress. Almost all forms of heart disease may lead to heart failure.

Causes: A heart attack that leaves a scar on the heart and interferes with the pumping of the heart causes CHF. Other causes are high blood pressure, atherosclerosis, arrhythmias, chronic lung disease, long-term drug intake, excessive alcohol intake and infections of the heart muscle or valves.

Those who have had a heart attack are more prone to CHF. The risk increases with advancing age.

Symptoms: Breathlessness, even with little exertion, swelling around the ankles and feet, irregular heart beat, fatigue, weakness, severe cough that produces reddish brown sputum, and chest pain, are some of the symptoms.

Treatment: This includes diagnosis of the underlying cause, rest, diuretic medicines, and diet, followed by brisk walking to improve the patient's condition.

Habits such as smoking and drinking, and a diet that is high in fats and use of excessive salt should be eliminated. Regular aerobic exercise like walking is recommended.

Peripheral Arterial Disease

This is a disease of the peripheral arteries, especially those in the legs and the arms.

Causes: The most common cause is the deposition of plaque in the arteries (atheroma). Other causes are a thrombus in the pulmonary artery, inflammatory diseases affecting blood vessels (vasculitis), and Raynaud's disease (a condition resulting from constriction of small blood vessels in response to severe cold or stress).

Men are more at risk than women among smokers, and the risk increases with age.

Symptoms: Discomfort and pain in the legs and buttocks which comes with walking and disappears with rest is indicative of this disease. Other symptoms are cold feet and discoloration of legs, feet and buttocks, loss of hair, small ulcers in the legs, which can later develop into gangrene.

Prevention: It is absolutely essential to give up smoking. It aggravates the onset of peripheral arterial diseases. Weight reduction is a must for the obese. Those most at risk should avoid drugs and foods that cause vasoconstriction, control diabetes and hypertension, do regular exercise and avoid infection and trauma.

CHAPTER 3

Diagnosing Heart Disease

There are many different tests for heart disease. You may already be familiar with some of the basic tests. The choice of the test depends on the risk factors, health history, and the symptoms. Tests usually start from the simplest and the non-invasive and progress to the more complicated.

All tests are interpreted by specialists and corelated with the history of the individual. Some of the more frequently used diagnostic tests are discussed briefly.

Electrocardiography (ECG): ECG is an important aid in diagnosing heart disease. In its simplest and most common form, it is simply a recording of the electrical activity of the heart. The electrical activity is detected by electrodes attached to the skin and is displayed as waves either on a strip of paper, or on a monitor. The variations in the waves can detect several abnormal conditions that affect the heart – including arrhythmias, ischaemia, coronary heart disease, myocardial infarction and hypertrophy or thickening of the heart muscles. ECG recordings also provide crucial information about previous heart attacks.

Exercise (Stress) ECG: Exercise or stress ECG is obtained while performing progressively increased level of exercise, usually on a treadmill. The recordings are taken before, during and after the exercise. A person is encouraged to exercise until too tired to continue, or shortness of breath, or chest pain is noticed. An exercise ECG is necessary to confirm the clinical diagnosis of ischaemic heart disease and is useful in guiding further management of arrhythmia.

Chest Radiograph (X-ray): A chest X-ray is useful in detecting heart enlargement, diseases of the pericardium, valvular heart disease, congestive heart failure and congenital heart disease problems.

Echocardiography (ECHO): Echocardiography is special application of diagnostic ultrasound to 'look' directly into the heart without any invasive procedure. The ultrasound waves are reflected or bounced back from the internal structures of the heart. A 'picture' of the heart is reconstructed on the basis of the reflected waves.

The echocardiogram can be obtained in various reflected ways—the M-mode echocardiogram, the 2-D echocardiogram, the Doppler ultrasound and the colour Doppler—depending on the information required.

The echocardiography enables the doctor to accurately observe and measure the heart size, its pumping strength, any heart muscle damage, any type of valve problem, structural abnormalities and blood pressure in the pulmonary arteries.

Angiocardiography: It involves injecting a contrast material (dye) into the blood vessels and imaging the flow on X-ray motion pictures or on videotape. It is used to detect coronary artery disease, heart valve defects, to identify partial or total blockages and to measure the blood flow within the blood vessels and the heart.

CT/CAT Scan: Both CT scan (computed tomography scan) and CAT (computerised axial tomography) scan use X-ray beams to generate images. Part of the X-ray machine is rotated rapidly around the body to obtain images from all angles. These images are combined by the computer to get a detailed cross-section image or picture. It allows the doctor to view internal structure of the heart including the pericardium, and the blood vessels. The information obtained is more comprehensive and accurate than from a simple X-ray.

MRI (Magnetic Resonance Imaging): This technique involves detection of small energy signals emitted by atoms of the body tissues to construct images. Because magnetic environment is used, some patients including those with pacemakers or other metallic implants cannot undergo MRI.

Radionuclide Scanning: This is a nuclear scanning technique. Trace amounts of radioactive material called radionuclides are injected into the blood stream. These "tracers" give off small amounts of radiation that are detected and processed by a computer to generate an image of how the material is distributed inside the body. Depending on the type of scanning, information can be gathered about the size of the heart chambers, their pumping abilities, and blood flow to the heart muscles and to the lungs.

Haemodynamic Monitoring: This involves using a special monitoring catheter inserted through a vein and threaded into the heart and the pulmonary artery. It measures pressure inside the heart and the artery and can detect any changes in the heart's pumping function.

Lipid (Blood Fat) Profile: Measurement of blood fat is necessary for all heart patients. Various blood constituents are measured not only to determine the presence of abnormal concentrations of lipids (blood fat), triglycerides, cholesterol and other related materials in the blood, but also to evaluate the effect of dietary changes and therapy on fat concentration. (See page 35)

Blood Pressure: High blood pressure seldom shows any symptoms. Being a high risk factor, measurement of blood pressure is one of the first steps in assessing the state of the heart and cardiovascular systems. (See page 45)

Blood Sugar: Blood glucose or blood sugar tests are done to determine the level of sugar concentration in the blood. High blood sugar levels indicate the presence of diabetes or a diabetic tendency, are both high risk factors for heart disease

CHAPTER 4

Understanding Dietary Risks

You can control some risk factors. Not all. The selection of foods to eat is a matter of your choice and control. Diet plays a far bigger role than other risk factor in influencing the health of the heart. A diet high in total fat, saturated fat and cholesterol can block the arteries and cause heart disease, especially coronary heart disease.

Before going into the details of dietary fat as a risk factor, it is important to go over the general information on fats.

What are Lipids?

The term lipid is applied to a group of naturally occurring fats (cholesterol and triglycerides) circulating in the blood stream. These fats are characterised by their insolubility in water and by their greasy feel.

Getting Your Fats Right

For the purpose of understanding, both fats and oils are categorised as 'fats'. Fats consist of fatty acids and glycerol. There are number of different essential fatty acids commonly present in foods. Without these essential fatty acids in our diet, heart and other health problems can occur.

Fats are not only a rich source of calories (1g of fat provides 9 kcal) but also essential for our well-being and good health. They carry the fat soluble vitamins A, D, E and K and are precursor of many hormones.

Visible and Invisible Fats: Fat in the diet is of two kinds: the visible and the invisible.

Visible fats are extracted from animals (fats like butter, *ghee*, etc.), from oil seeds (vegetable oils), and from fish (fish oil).

Invisible fats occur in all foods, especially milk, milk products like curd, cream, cheese and cottage cheese and in eggs, vegetables, fruits and spices. Increased intake of both visible and invisible fats contribute to heart disease.

Excess of fat, whether visible or invisible, in the diet is a major risk factor for heart disease.

A more meaningful classification of fats from dietary point of view is into saturated fats and unsaturated fats.

Saturated Fats: Saturated fat is mostly found in foods of animal origin such as milk, butter, cheese, cream, *ghee* and meat. Some vegetable oils such as palm oil and coconut oil are also rich in saturated fat. Saturated fats tend to be solid at room temperature; that is an easy way to identify saturated fat.

In India, unlike in the West, where the largest source of saturated fat is red meat, large amounts of saturated fat are consumed through high intake of butter and *ghee* – both *desi ghee* and vegetable *ghee* or *vanaspati.* Many people take great pride in cooking only in *desi ghee*.

Vegetable *ghee* (like Dalda, Rath and other brands) is another cooking medium widely used in India and other South Asian countries. This is manufactured by hydrogenation of vegetable oils (i.e. by adding hydrogen to vegetable oils). This converts the liquid oils into semi-solid fats and greatly increases the saturation of the fatty acids.

High intake of saturated fat is an often-seen cause of heart disease. It is a potent dietary risk factor. Saturated fats raise the total blood cholesterol, as well as LDL cholesterol (the bad cholesterol) and lower the HDL cholesterol (the good cholesterol). This risk gets multiplied manifold if other risk factors like obesity, alcohol consumption, diabetes etc. are present.

Unsaturated Fats: Unsaturated fats remain liquid at room temperature and are found in vegetable oils. They are far less harmful as compared to saturated fats and are a good source of all essential fatty acids.

Numerous scientific studies have confirmed that judicious use of unsaturated fats lowers high blood cholesterol and reduces the probability of heart disease.

Unsaturated fats are of two kinds–monounsaturated and polyunsaturated. Good sources of monounsaturated fats are olive, canola, almond, rapeseed, mustard and groundnut oil. In the Mediterranean region, where olive oil is widely used, the incidence of heart disease is considerably lower than in other European countries. It has been confirmed that olive oil protects the heart by lowering total blood cholesterol, in particular the LDL cholesterol, raising HDL cholesterol (the good cholesterol) and leaving triglycerides level unchanged.

Polyunsaturated fats are found in sunflower oil, corn oil and soyabean oil. Sesame oil and rice bran oil are a mixture of monounsaturated and polyunsaturated fats.

Fish Oil: The Omega-3 advantage

In the recent years a number of scientific studies have confirmed that consumption of fish and fish oils can reduce the likelihood of a heart attack.

Fish oils are the fats extracted from fish and shell fish, particularly fatty cold water fish like salmon, mackarel and herring. Among the wide variety of fatty acids present in fish oil are Omega-3 polyunsaturated fatty acids.

Omega-3 fatty acids reduce the tendency of formation of blood clots, lower LDL and increase HDL. These fatty acids reduce the chances of narrowing of blood vessels and protect the heart from atherosclerosis. They also decrease the production of triglycerides in the liver and regulate blood pressure.

Omega-3 fatty acids are also available from foods such as flaxseed, canola oil, green leafy vegetables, soyabeans and nuts. These foods contain polyunsaturated fat that the body can convert to Omega-3 fatty acid.

The Fatty Acid Content in Common Fats and Oils (g/100g)

	Fat Content	Saturated(S)	MUFA(M)**	PUFA(P)**	Cholesterol mg*/100g*	Predominant Fatty Acid
Butter	81	50	23	8	250	S
Coconut oil	100	90	7	3	0	S
Corn oil	100	12	32	56	0	P
Ghee	100	65	32	3	300	S
Groundnut oil	100	24	50	26	0	M
Vanaspati (Hydrogenated Fats)	100	35	20	5	0	S
Lard	100	40	46	12	92	S
Margarine	79	14	29	35	0	M+P
Olive oil	100	13	76	11	0	M
Palm oil	100	45	44	11	0	S+M
Rapeseed/mustard oil	100	8	70	22	0	M
Red Palm oil	100	50	40	10	0	S+M
Rice bran oil	100	22	41	37	0	M+P
Safflower	100	13	27	60	0	P
Sesame	100	15	42	43	0	M+P
Soyabean	100	15	27	58	0	P
Sunflower	100	13	27	60	0	P

*g-gram **MUFA-monounsaturated fatty acid
mg- milligram PUFA-polyunsaturated fatty acid

Source: National Institute of Nutrition, Hyderabad

Balancing Saturated and Unsaturated Fats: Without a proper balance of saturated and unsaturated fats, the membranes are either too solid or too fluid and cell integrity is lost. In other words, excessive intake of any one kind of fat should be avoided. A combination of oils is necessary to get the correct balance.

A ratio of polyunsaturated fat to saturated fat of 1:05 prevents coronary heart disease.

What is Cholesterol?

Cholesterol, one of the several types of lipids (fats) present in the blood, is essential for our survival. It is an important building block for body cells and certain hormones. Liver cannot function effectively without the presence of cholesterol in the body. However, as potent as it is to maintain life, it is equally dangerous and life threatening when out of proportion in our body.

The human body makes its own cholesterol. The amount of cholesterol manufactured by the body is sufficient to carry out its important metabolic functions.

Eating cholesterol rich foods can lead to higher-than-desirable levels of blood cholesterol, which then leads to atherosclerosis and to coronary heart disease. It is important to remember that cholesterol is found only in foods derieved from animal, and not plant, sources.

A number of research studies have confirmed a direct relationship between increased blood (serum) lipid levels (cholesterol and triglycerides) and the incidence of heart disease, especially atherosclerosis and coronary heart disease.

What are Triglycerides?

Triglycerides, like cholesterol, is a type of fat present in the blood. The body digests the fat in the food and releases triglycerides into the blood. The liver also changes excess calories into triglycerides. Research suggests that elevated triglycerides may contribute to coronary heart disease.

What are Lipoproteins?

Lipoproteins are the vehicles that carry cholesterol and triglycerides, both of which are water insoluble, from the liver through blood circulation to different parts of the body. Total cholesterol is the sum total of cholesterol carried by lipoproteins.

The main types of lipoproteins which carry cholesterol are:

- Low Density Lipoprotein Cholesterol (LDL)
- High Density Lipoprotein Cholestero (HDL)
- Very Low Density Lipoprotein (VLDL) contain mostly triglycerides, and only small amounts of cholesterol.

These three lipoproteins play a major role in heart disease. Abnormalities in the circulating lipoproteins is a risk factor for development of coronary heart disease.

Good Cholesterol, Bad Cholesterol

LDL—The Bad Cholesterol: The LDL or the Low Density Lipoproteins, are the primary transport vehicle for cholesterol. LDL cholesterol is more likely to cause atherosclerosis because it carries cholesterol into the arterial wall, resulting in the build up of plaques which block the arteries. The higher the LDL cholesterol in the blood, the greater is the risk of heart disease. If the LDL cholesterol level is above 130 mg/dL, the person is at increased risk for heart disease. Research indicates that higher levels of LDL cholesterol reflect a defective transportation system that leads to atherosclerosis.

HDL—The Good Cholesterol: The HDL or the High Density Lipoproteins contain less cholesterol than LDL. These liporoteins have a protective effect on the heart; they remove cholesterol from the arteries and carry it away to the liver before it can be deposited on the arterial walls. But if HDL-cholesterol levels are below 40 mg/dL then the person is at increased risk for heart disease. Higher levels of HDL cholesterol reflect a healthy transportation system and do not lead to athersclerosis. This is the reason the HDL cholesterol is called 'good cholesterol' and LDL cholesterol is known as the 'bad cholesterol'.

Fats, Food and Cholesterol

The influence of fat on cholesterol depends on the degree of saturation. Depending on the extent of saturation, the LDL and HDL levels are influenced in different ways. Saturated fatty acids tend to elevate the total cholesterol levels as well as LDL cholesterol, and lower the HDL cholesterol levels.

Foods that increase cholesterol: Foods that contain cholesterol, saturated fats and hydrogenated fats increase the blood cholesterol levels. These foods put an extra load on the liver and kidneys to clear the blood of the substances that result from fat digestion. Whether taken in moderation or in excess, these foods are potential risk factors for heart disease. (See pages 73-74).

Other dietary factors that increase cholesterol: A number of other dietary factors also raise blood cholesterol levels. Some people are sensitive to excess carbohydrates. These people respond with a temporary increase in triglyceride and lower HDL cholesterol levels. Generally, heart patients who are obese or diabetic, and have impaired glucose tolerance, show this response.

Increased intake of foods or increased intake of calories is also a

Safe and High Levels of Blood Cholesterol

By far the most comprehensive and widely accepted classification of healthy and unhealthy total cholesterol levels has been issued by the US National Cholesterol Education Programme.

Desirable	—	less than 200 mg/dL
Borderline-high	—	200-239 mg/dL
High	—	more than 240 mg/dL

Besides total cholesterol, three other measurements relating to LDL, HDL and trigylycerides are important. LDL cholesterol above 130 mg/dL and HDL cholesterol below 35 mg/dL, and total cholesterol above 200 mg/dL are at greater risk for heart diseases. Triglyceride levels above 250 mg/dL are a significant risk.

dietary risk factor for heart disease. Refined foods including sugars are more atherogenic. Large amounts of animal protein are also a dietary risk factor.

Too much salt can modify and accelerate the other major risk factors such as diabetes, hypertension and hyperlipidemia. People who consume more than 10g of salt a day are at increased risk.

Research indicates that soft water (as compared to hard water), increases the risk of heart disease. Being more acidic it is more likely to dissolve the toxic trace elements from pipes and rocks. Moreover it has low levels of calcium, and therefore may not provide protection for the heart.

What reduces HDL cholesterol? Low HDL cholesterol is a risk factor for heart disease. Apart from saturated fats, hydrogenated fats and cholesterol rich foods, a number of other factors also reduce HDL cholesterol. They are obesity, lack of exercise, heavy cigarette smoking, use of steroids, increased triglyceride levels and genetic factors. High carbohydrate diets also lower HDL cholesterol.

However, not all persons with low HDL cholesterol are at risk. Many vegetarians are generally accustomed to very low fat diets which lower both the LDL cholesterol and the HDL cholesterol. Such people usually are not at risk, since their increased intake of whole grain cereals, legumes, fruits and vegetables protects the heart. However, even such

Why are Some People at Higher Risk from Dietary Fats?

Some people appear to have a powerful endogenous feedback system that responds to dietary intakes of cholesterol by regulating liver synthesis. Dietary cholesterol in such people does not raise blood cholesterol levels. But in people who have less sensitive endogenous feedback systems, dietary cholesterol causes a rapid rise in blood cholesterol levels.

Similarly, people who are SFA (saturated fatty acid) sensitive respond to SFA with much higher elevations of blood cholesterol than those who are not sensitive.

individuals are at an increased risk if there is a fami y history of heart disease, or they smoke and drink.

The right diet helps to keep the arteries clear and reduces the risk of heart problems and stroke.

Calories, Diet and Healthy Heart

Carbohydrates, proteins and fat found in foods and alcohol provide calories (energy provided by food is measured in calories). Fat provides more than twice the calories per weight of carbohydrates or protein. That is why reducing fat intake is an effective way to trim calories.

All fats – saturated, nonunsaturated and polyunsaturated – provide the same amount of calories. Therefore, while polyunsaturated oils maybe safer for the heart, yet excess intake is harmful because it increases the total intake of calories.

Your daily calorie requirement*: The following is approx. number of calories needed to maintain weight depending on the kind of work.

	Men (Body wt. 60kg)	*Women (Body wt. 50kg)*
Sedentary work	2425 kcal	1875 kcal
Moderate work	2875 kcal	2225 kcal
Heavy work	3800 kcal	2925 kcal

It is generally recommended that these calories should be derieved from different food sources to maintain balance between health, energy and protection against disease.

	Normal Diet	*Low Fat Diet*
Carbohydrates	55-65%	less than 70%
Protein	20-25%	15%
Fat	15-20%	15%

Are low fat diets recommended? According to American Heart Association Science Advisory of May, 1998, while results from few clinical trials suggest that very low fat diets are associated with reduced

* Source: National Institute of Nutrition, Hyderabad.

What the American Heart Association says...

There is overwhelming evidence that reduction in saturated fat, dietary cholesterol and weight is the most effective dietary strategy for reducing total cholesterol, LDL-C levels, and cardiovascular risk. ... there is no biological requirement for saturated fat. Essential fatty acids can be adequately derived from unsaturated sources even if total fat intake is less than 15% of total calories, but the appropriate types and amounts of the dietary fat sources must be selected i.e. high polyunsaturated vegetable oils.

Am. Heart Association, Science Advisory, 1998, May

risk of cardiovascular disease, there remain numerous unanswered questions. That makes recommendations of such diet premature.

Similarly zero-fat diets cannot be recommended. Certain amount of fat, especially PUFA is a must in the diet. It supplies the essential fatty acids that plays significant role in a number of physiological body functions.

CHAPTER 5

Lifestyle *and other* Risk Factors

Some individuals, inspite of a healthy lifestyle, are at a greater risk for heart diseases due to genetic or inherited factors. But in the majority of people it is the lifestyle induced stress and anxiety, with cravings for food and starvation diets, sedentary habits, smoking, excessive intake of alcohol and too much tea and coffee, that increases risk for heart diseases. These risk factors are not directly related to diet or to intake of fat, and are referred to as non-lipid related risk factors.

Non-lipid related risk factors may broadly be categorised as uncontrollable and controllable.

Uncontrollable Risk Factors

Gender and age: Men are more prone to heart disease than women. Early heart attacks occur predominantly in men. Among men the incidence and mortality due to heart disease approximately doubles in each 5-year period after the age of 24 years. The rate of heart disease is 3 to 4 times higher in men than in women during middle age, and twice as high in the elderly. Women have relatively few cardiovascular diseases during the childbearing years; they are protected by the hormone estrogen. However, after menopause, incidence of heart disease among women is about the same as in men.

Heredity: Some families are more prone to heart disease than others; genetically their serum cholesterol and lipoprotein concentrations are on the higher side. Such families also often have higher incidence of other diseases, such as hypertension, diabetes mellitus, gout and hyperlipidemia. These conditions are also independent risk factors for various heart diseases.

Controllable Risk Factors

Non-lipid controllable risk factors for heart disease are lifestyle factors such as stress and anxiety, poor breathing habits, sedentary daily living, smoking, excessive intake of alcohol, tea and coffee and conditions such as hypertension, diabetes mellitus and obesity. To prevent heart disease, all controllable risk factors should be minimised or eliminated; merely eliminating one or two factors is not the solution.

Tension, Stress and Heart Disease

We live in the most tension packed era in the history of humankind; some degree of tension and stress are a part of our daily life. It is an old observation that tension or stress disrupt the normal working of the body, and can lead to different diseases.

Stress is an important risk factor in the development of heart disease; perhaps the most important. Stress may be emotional, occupational, social, cultural, hereditary or physical. In addition to genetic predisposition, weak organs, unhealthy behaviour, personality patterns and a fast work pace also cause stress.

Stressful living often leads to cravings and binge eating of high calorie and saturated fatty foods like cakes, sweets, fried snacks etc. These in turn lead to obesity, hypertension, diabetes and increased blood cholesterol levels, which are all risk factors for heart disease.

Are Indians More at Risk?

Research shows that Indians are more prone to heart disease because they are genetically inclined towards increased cholesterol levels. The high intake of dietary fats specially saturated fats like *ghee* and *vanaspati*, and sugars contribute significantly to high incidence of heart disease.

Research shows that even in the absence of cravings and binge eating, blood cholesterol levels rise during stressful periods. This indicates that lipid-regulating mechanisms are responsive to stress. Muscles provide the first tell-tale signs of mounting tension and anxiety which cause the heart to beat faster, the blood pressure to go up, and the arteries to go into spasm. This ultimately leads to heart problems.

Prolonged periods of stress also cause increased cardiac output which results in hypertension. Hypertension, in turn, leads to the weakening and tearing of the linings of the blood vessels, thus providing a focal point for the deposition of cholesterol plaques on the blood vessel lining and narrowing of the lumen of the vessels.

Stress also causes the loss of some nutrients like protein, vitamin A, some B complex vitamins, vitamin C, K and potassium, all necessary for various physiological functions. Stress, therefore, affects not only mental but also physical health.

Poor Breathing Habits

There is a critical relationship between breathing and cardiovascular functioning.

Many of us, knowingly or unknowingly, develop poor breathing habits such as shallow breathing, irregular breathing with uneven inhalation and exhalation cycles, frequent holding of breath, breathing through the mouth, or chest breathing (caused by emotional disturbance, or poor posture, or tight clothing) where only the upper portion of the chest shows motion. These incorrect breathing patterns create stress and heart problems. One example of a deadly breathing pattern is the sustained and regular pattern of apnea, or the involuntary retention of breath, commonly found in heart patients.

The way we breathe has an effect on the electrical activity of the heart. Research indicates that those who suffer a heart attack due to arrhythmia can really be said to have more of a breathing problem than a heart problem.

It is, therefore, important to develop correct habit of breathing using the diaphragm. The diaphragm plays an important role in breathing. With each inhalation of breath it contracts and moves downwards, thus expanding the chest cavity and enabling the lungs to fill in air. With each expiration, the diaphragm relaxes and pushes up, decreasing the chest cavity and forcing the air out of the lungs.

Sedentary Living is Risky

The rapid mechanisation of everyday life has promoted sedentary living. The affluent and the less affluent, the better and the less educated, the overweight and the obese, women, people who are physically and mentally challenged, all exhibit a high level of sedentary behaviour. Leisure time is spent in watching TV and simultaneously eating high calorie snacks, rather than on outdoor activity.

Sedentary lifestyle is a major risk factor not only for heart disease but for a host of other health problems. As a risk factor for heart diseases, it ranks at par with cigarette smoking, high blood pressure and elevated cholesterol levels.

People who lead sedentary lives have low cardio-vascular fitness and run about twice the risk of developing heart disease compared to the physically active. Moreover, sedentary persons with other risk factors like smoking, high blood pressure and high cholesterol levels, are even more prone to heart disease.

A physically active life which includes the recommended physical activity of 20 to 30 minutes of regular moderate aerobic exercise 3 to 4 times a week reduces the risk of heart disease drastically.

Smoking: Doubling your risk

Smokers are high risk candidates for heart attacks. The risk of a smoker dying from coronary heart disease is two to three times greater than that of a non-smoker. The risk increases with the number of cigarettes smoked as well as the duration of smoking.

Tobacco smoke has three main components: nicotine, tar and carbon monoxide. Nicotine increases the heartbeat and the heart's demand for oxygen. Tar from burning tobacco coats the lungs and reduces the elasticity of the tiny air sacs which impairs oxygen absorption into the bloodstream. Carbon monoxide in the tobacco smoke reduces the supply of oxygen carried by the blood to the heart and other muscles.

Smoking thus results in the absorption of nicotine and carbon monoxide in the bloodstream, which may cause an increase in the blood pressure and the heart rate. It may also contribute towards atherosclerosis and thrombosis.

Finally, there is no such thing as moderate smoking. Each cigarette has the potential to trigger a heart disease.

Passive smoking: Smoking affects the health not only of smokers but also of non-smokers in the vicinity; the unfiltered smoke inhaled by non-smokers is more hazardous than the smoke inhaled by smokers. It contains five times more carbon monoxide, four times more tar and nicotine, and forty times more carcinogens, than the smoke that is inhaled from a cigarette. In poorly ventilated areas, carbon monoxide levels in the blood are the same in smokers and non-smokers. Heart patients who are non-smokers should avoid places where there is heavy concentration of cigarette smoke.

Alcohol

Medical research has established a strong link between alcohol consumption and hypertension: the more you drink, the higher the blood pressure. Research has linked a whole range of organ breakdowns involving the heart, blood vessels, kidneys, liver and nerves to alcohol. Even moderate drinkers tend to have enlarged hearts, high blood pressure and poor heart reserve in times of crisis. Alcohol also increases the triglyceride levels in the blood.

Alcohol has zero nutrition content and provides only calories. Too much alcohol can make a person feel full and displace more nutritious foods from the diet, causing nutritional deficiencies harmful for the heart.

People who overindulge in alcohol tend to be obese; the excess alcohol calories are converted into fat. The body takes one hour to burn 7g of alcohol. Binge drinking can cause abnormalities in heart rhythms, leading to possible alcohol induced cardiac failure, or alcoholic heart diseases.

Exercise doesn't really help the body to eliminate alcohol as it does in the case of other high calorie foods. It would be fair to say that alcohol is best avoided.

Tea and Coffee: Do they affect your heart?

Both tea and coffee contain caffeine. Caffeine is perhaps the most widely used mood elevator in the world; it decreases fatigue and tiredness and helps the body work more efficiently till the effect wears off. Soft drinks like Pepsi and Coca Cola also contain caffeine.

It is known that excessive caffeine causes nervousness, anxiety, loss of appetite, sleeplessness, and increase in blood pressure. It makes the heart beat faster and can cause irregular heartbeats. Caffeine intake has also been linked to high cholesterol levels and increased risk of CHD.

Between tea and coffee, health promoters put forward that tea is perhaps a better drink since its caffeine content is lower and the bioflavanoids present in it have antioxidant properties.

In most parts of the world, both regular coffee and decaffeinated coffee are available. It is generally assumed that decaffeinated coffee is less harmful. That is only partly true. Research has established that decaffeinated coffee tends to raise blood cholesterol levels more than regular coffee.

A Toast to Your Health?

Many studies show that moderate alcohol consumption lowers the risk of heart disease, specially for those in their middle ages. It appears to raise levels of good cholesterol and may help in preventing blood clots. It has even been suggested that alcohol tends to open up arteries.

There is no unanimity on whether wine is superior to beer or liqour, although some studies suggest that wine has more beneficial compounds. No matter what you prefer, do ask your doctor for guidelines. Until researchers know more about how alcohol affects health, it is best to drink in moderation. And with meals. Food slows alcohol absorption.

It would therefore be safe to say that tea is less harmful than coffee; and instant coffee is preferable to brewed, percolated and decaffeinated coffee. Finally, while one or two cups of tea/coffee a day are safe, excessive intake of caffeine is potentially harmful.

Hypertension: A high risk factor

Hypertension is a medical term for high blood pressure. When the body system is not able to regulate the blood pressure the way it is supposed to, the pressure of the blood in the arteries increases. A consistently higher than normal pressure over a long period of time is called high blood pressure.

The blood pressure is called high if the systolic pressure is 140 mm Hg or higher, and the diastolic pressure is 90 mm Hg or higher, or both.

There are three stages of high blood pressure based on severity. These stages are referred to as stages 1, 2 and 3. Innumerable research studies have established a direct relationship between high blood pressure and coronary heart disease, heart attack, stroke and heart failure.

Hypertension also encourages the development of atherosclerosis possibly by weakening the arterial wall with exertion of pressure at susceptible points and opening it to invasion by lipids and other materials.

High Blood Pressure: How High is High? **

	Systolic (mm Hg)		Diastolic (mm Hg)
Optimal*	120 or less	and	80 or less
Normal	129 or less	and	84 or less
High-normal	130-139	or	85-89
Hypertension			
Stage 1	140-159	or	90-99
Stage 2	160-179	or	100-109
Stage 3	180 or higher	or	110 or higher

* Optimal pressure with respect to cardiovascular risk.

**Source: National Institute of Health, USA. The Sixth Report of the Joint National Committee on Prevention, Detection, Evaluation, & Treatment of High Blood Pressure, 1997.

Heredity, obesity, excess sodium, low levels of calcium, potassium and magnesium, increased intake of saturated and hydrogenated fats, smoking, alcohol, some medications and physical inactivity are the risk factors for hypertension.

Diabetes and Your Heart

Diabetes, or diabetes mellitus, is a major risk factor in coronary heart disease and peripheral vascular disease.

Normally the food we eat is converted by the body into glucose or sugar which provides energy. The presence of glucose in the blood is regulated by insulin. Insulin also helps in utilisation and storage of glucose by the body. In diabetes, an absolute or relative lack of insulin results in the body not being able to use glucose properly and instead the glucose levels increase beyond the normal in the blood.

Prolonged high sugar levels in the blood damage the blood vessels and make them more vulnerable to disease.

Moreover, in the absence of insulin or effective insulin activity, lipolysis (splitting of fats) is promoted and free fatty acids, triglycerides, cholesterol and phospholipids increase in the blood, leading to atherosclerosis and coronary heart disease. Therefore, the risk of heart disease among diabetics is 2 to 3 times higher than in non-diabetics.

Obesity: An acquired risk

The obese generally tend to have elevated levels of cholesterol and triglycerides, high blood pressure and poor cardio-vascular health. Hypertension in obesity has a strong relationship to high lipid levels which can lead to a number of cardio-vascular abnormalities. This puts the obese in high risk category for coronary heart disease and other related complications. The risk of CHD is three times greater for the middle aged obese males as compared to the non-obese.

Mortality due to coronary heart disease and stroke among the obese is also influenced by regional fat distribution. Abdominal obesity, also referred to as apple-shaped, is more dangerous than the hip obesity. If most of the extra weight is below the waist, around the hip and thigh, it is called pear-shaped obesity. Generally it is better to have a pear-shape than the shape of an apple. The fat around the abdomen tends to accumulate in the artery and increases the risk of coronary heart disease, high blood pressure, diabetes and stroke.

The mortality rate due to coronary heart disease and stroke also increases with increased waist/hip ratio (WHR). The ideal WHR for men is 1:1 (waist:hip) and for women 0.8:1. Lower is not harmful, but a higher ratio does reflect increased risk.

Obesity also causes adverse alterations in metabolism or hormone complications such as hyper insulinemia, insulin resistance, hypertension and non-insulin dependent diabetes.

High cholesterol among the obese is directly related to the incidence of atherosclerosis in the coronary arteries. This can lead to thrombosis or a massive heart attack.

The obese also have higher incidence of impaired glucose tolerance and greater risk of type-2 diabetes. The diabetic obese are four times more prone to coronary heart disease than the non diabetic and non obese.

Body Mass Index (BMI) and Heart Disease

A good way of determining whether you are overweight or not is to look at your Body Mass Index. Body Mass Index factors both your height and weight in determining excess weight.

$$\text{Body Mass Index} = \frac{\text{Weight in kg}}{(\text{Height in metres})^2}$$

The result is compared with the table below:

	Ideal	*Overweight*	*Obese*
BMI for Men	17-25	25-30	more than 30
BMI for Women	17-27	27-32	more than 32

There is an increased risk of coronary heart disease and stroke with increased BMI mainly among smokers and diabetics. A higher intake of dietary fat results in increased BMI.

CHAPTER 6

The Heart Protectors Antioxidants, Vitamins and Minerals

The heart muscle, like any other body tissue, is dependent on an adequate supply of essential nutrients. Generally malnourished or under nourished people show cardiac impairment. Semi-starvation diets which tend to deliver incomplete nourishment also affect the normal functioning of the heart; they cause weight loss, lower the metabolic rate, decrease the blood pressure and pulse rate, and lead to changes in the heart size.

A balanced intake of nutrients is, therefore, essential for maintaining a healthy heart.

Antioxidants and Free Radicals

One of the most important medical advances of the last fifty years is the new understanding of the way in which the human body is damaged and weakened, making it susceptible to a wide range of diseases, including heart disease. The essence of this knowledge is that the damage to our cells and tissues is at the root of most diseases. This damage is caused by highly active and dangerous chemical groups called 'free radicals.' Free radicals are constantly being formed in the body as a result of basic disease processes. They are also formed by exposure to toxic chemicals, cigarette smoke, car exhaust, industrial fumes and all forms of radiation, including exposure to rays of the sun or due to various metabolic processes which accompany ageing.

All this would be of academic interest only were it not for the fact that research has shown that free radicals can be effectively combated. This is where antioxidant vitamins come in.

How do Antioxidants Protect?

For many years now, scientists have known that free radicals can be controlled or even prevented by a range of antioxidant substances. Fortunately, the human body has its own antioxidants for damage limitation. There are enzymes and nutrients in the blood which mop up free radicals before they have a chance to do any harm to body tissues and organs. These protective substances – called the antioxidants – include vitamins A, C and E, beta carotene, a plant pigment with antioxidant properties. In addition, many minerals like iron, zinc, copper, selenium, and manganese, also have antioxidant properties.

A diet rich in vitamins A, C and E, beta-carotene, selenium, alpha lipoic acid (ALA) and coenzyme Q10, gives protection not only from heart disease but also from cancer. These antioxidants remove the free radicals and ...reduce the oxidative stress harmful to the heart.

Where to Find Antioxidants in Your Food

Phytochemicals: These are chemical substances found in almost all fruits and vegetables. These phytochemicals have antioxidant properties which benefit people suffering from hypertension, circulatory problems and heart diseases. They are more abundant in cruciferous vegetables (related to plants of the cabbage family) such as Brussels sprouts, broccoli, cabbage, cauliflower, kale and turnips.

Bioflavonoids are phytochemicals found in citrus fruits, plums, cherries, black berries, black currants, apple, onion, green tea, soya beans and in red wine. In the body they work with vitamin C to strengthen the small blood vessels or capillaries. Flavonoids being potent antioxidants reduce the risk of heart disease. People who get sufficient flavonoids in their diet have a reduced risk of heart disease.

Plant pigments: Plant pigments also have antioxidant properties. Carotenoids, a group of pigments related to vitamin A, are found in orange, red, and yellow coloured fruits and vegetables like mango, papaya and carrot, strawberries, cherries, blue berries, raspberries, grapes, black currants, beetroot, tomatoes, pumpkins, musk melon, and red peppers and dark green vegetables.

Research has shown that foods rich in carotenoids have anti-oxidant properties and reduce the risk of heart disease by preventing the formation of LDL cholesterol. In fact, some pigments found in black currants and blue berries also have anti-bacterial and anti-inflammatory properties.

Vitamins Help

Vitamins are organic compounds. Though required in small amounts, they are essential for the proper functioning of the body. Because vitamins act in association with enzymes and only tiny quantities are required, the daily requirement is nearly always present in a reasonably balanced diet.

Some vitamins, in addition to their other physiological role, also play an important role in protecting the heart. These vitamins act as biological antioxidants, and the most prominent among these are vitamins C and E.

Vitamins can be broadly divided as fat soluble vitamins and water-soluble vitamins.

Water soluble vitamins: Vitamins (vitamin B-complex and vitamin C) dissolve easily in water. A portion of these vitamins may actually be destroyed by heating or cooking. They cannot be stored in the body and need to be taken daily. Any excess intake of these vitamins is eliminated as waste. The B-complex group of vitamins is essential for blood circulation and to keep the heart healthy.

Fat soluble vitamins: Vitamins A, D, E and K are soluble in fat and fat solvents, and therefore categorised as fat soluble vitamins. They are not easily lost in cooking, and can generally be stored in the body, mostly in the liver.

Vitamin A: Being an antioxidant, vitamin A protects the heart. It reduces the risk of heart disease by preventing LDL cholesterol from damaging the heart and the coronary vessels.

Vitamin E: It is a powerful antioxidant which protects by reducing the harmful effects of LDL cholesterol. It prevents the formation of blood clots, reduces inflammation associated with heart disease and reduces the angina pain. It also helps in strengthening the peripheral circulatory system. Deficiency of this vitamin leads to the degeneration of the coronary system, stroke and other heart diseases.

Vitamin B_1 (Thiamine): It protects the heart muscles, helps maintain the normal red blood count, improves circulation and prevents oedema or fluid retention. In people with congestive heart failure, thiamine can improve the pumping power of the heart. It is useful in preventing constipation.

Vitamin B_3 (Niacin): This vitamin is required for proper circulation of blood. High doses of this vitamin with other B-complex vitamins afford relief from high blood pressure caused by high cholesterol and atherosclerosis. It lowers the total cholesterol, LDL cholesterol and triglycerides, while increasing the HDL cholesterol. Its deficiency leads to depression, insomnia and anaemia.

Vitamin B_5 (Pantothenic acid). A deficiency of this vitamin causes blood disorders.

Vitamin B_6 (Pyridoxine): A deficiency of this vitamin leads to heart disease and stroke. Vitamin B_6 works with folic acid and vitamin B_{12} and helps the body to process homocysteine, an amino acid like compound that has been linked to increased risk of heart disease, plaque build-up and clogging of arteries. High doses of this vitamin help in the treatment of blood clots in heart attack.

Vitamin B_9 (Folic acid): This reduces the risk of heart disease and stroke. It is necessary for the proper formation of red blood cells. Deficiency of this vitamin causes anaemia and impaired circulation.

Vitamin B_{12} (Cobolamin): Essential for the production and regeneration of red blood cells, vitamin B_{12} with folic acid helps the body to process homocysteine and thus lowers the risk of heart diseases. Its deficiency causes anaemia.

Vitamin C: This is a powerful antioxidant and protects the heart. It is required to absorb iron from other foods.

The Role of Minerals

Minerals are inorganic nutrients that are required for normal health. Some minerals are required by the body in substantial amounts, while others are needed in trace amounts and therefore called trace elements.

Apart from their many other functions, minerals play an important role in keeping blood and tissue fluid from becoming either too acidic or too alkaline. A number of minerals have a beneficial effect on the heart.

Calcium: It plays an important role in the contractions of the heart. It is also required to reduce the risk of hypertension.

When preparing a diet, it must be remembered that the availability of calcium is much higher in curd than in milk.

Iron: Iron finds place in the composition of haemoglobin. It distributes oxygen inhaled into the lungs to all the cells. Its deficiency causes anaemia.

Phosphorus: This mineral helps to maintain the acid base balance of the blood. Calcium cannot function unless phosphorus is also present. However, too much phosphorus in the diet affects the absorption of calcium and magnesium and therefore moderation is the key in dietetics.

Sulphur: Another mineral that helps to maintain the acid-base balance of the blood is sulphur.

Magnesium: A mineral that promotes a healthier cardio-vascular system, magnesium calms the nervous system thereby preventing stress and strain. It is involved in the production of lecithin which prevents the build-up of cholesterol and consequent atherosclerosis. Magnesium also inhibits blood clots, widens arteries and reduces the potential for arrhythmia (irregular heart beat). It also helps in lowering high blood pressure.

Sodium: Though sodium helps to maintain the acid base equilibrium

Vitamins that Protect the Heart

Vitamin A	Milk fat, beta-carotene orange, yellow and green fruits and vegetables, red, green and yellow peppers, green leafy vegetables, carrot, Brussels sprouts, broccoli, kale, asparagus, yam, sweet potato, pumpkin, mango, papaya, fresh and dried apricots and melons.
Vitamin B_1	Milk yeast, outer layer of whole grains, cereals, pulses, bean sprouts, green leafy vegetables, banana, apple, egg white, nuts especially Brazil nuts, and seeds.
Vitamin B_3	Whole wheat, green leafy vegetables, tomatoes, egg white, poultry, fish, dates, figs and prunes.
Vitamin B_5	Whole grain breads, cereals, green vegetables, peas, beans, and peanuts.
Vitamin B_6	Milk yeast, bran, pulses, cereals, bean sprouts, fresh vegetables, banana, avocados, egg white, walnuts and chestnut.
Vitamin B_9	Yeast, green leafy vegetables, broccoli, Brussels sprouts, bean sprouts, cabbage, beetroot, cucumber, mushrooms, artichokes, asparagus, berries, Italian chestnuts and water chestnuts.
Vitamin B_{12}	Milk, lean meat.
Vitamin C	Green leafy vegetables, broccoli, asparagus, cauliflower, kale, beetroots, sweet potato, tomatoes, Brussels sprouts, sprouted grams, citrus fruits, peaches, pineapple, papaya, guavas, gooseberries, apples, cherries, avocados, pears, strawberries, kiwi fruit, raspberries, mangoes, custard apples, lichees, pomegranate, dates and black currant.
Vitamin E	Milk, whole grain products, wheat germ, green leafy vegetables, sprouts, tofu, cabbage, asparagus, tomato, olives, avocado, nuts, sunflower seeds, vegetable oils.

in the body, its excessive use causes oedema, high blood pressure, hardening of the arteries and other heart diseases.

Potassium: Potassium controls the working of the vascular system and helps in regulating the heart-beat and the blood pressure. It is also important because it keeps the proper acid base balance of the blood and the tissues.

Deficiency of potassium causes abnormal heart beats, breathing difficulties and increases the risk of stroke. However, moderation is important; excessive intake of potassium slows the heart beat. Being a diuretic, diet rich in potassium reduces hypertension.

Chlorine: It regulates the acid base balance of the blood. It prevents building of excessive fat and autointoxication.

Trace Elements

As mentioned earlier, some minerals are required in such minute quantities that they are commonly referred to as trace elements. Although required in infinitely small quantities yet they have a vital role in healthy functioning of the body and cardio-vascular system. These minerals include chromium, cobalt, copper, manganese, selenium, silicon and zinc.

Copper is a powerful antioxidant which stimulates the growth of red blood cells. Selenium works with vitamin E in preventing cardio-vascular diseases like cardiomyopathy and hypertension. It reduces the stickiness of the blood and decreases the risk of clotting. Deficiency of selenium can cause degeneration of heart muscle. Research indicates that chromium helps to breakdown fats, lowers blood cholesterol and thus reduces the risk of heart disease.

Lecithin

Lecithin, is a phospholipid (a lipid containing phosphorous) commonly found in food. Scientific studies have shown that lecithin has the ability to break up cholesterol into small particles and thus prevent its deposition on the walls of the arteries and the veins. Lecithin also helps the cells to remove fats and cholesterol from the blood and to utilize

Minerals that Protect the Heart	
Calcium	Milk, milk products, whole wheat, leafy vegetables, young ones of various fishes—sardines, anchovies and herring, where the flesh and the bones are eaten together, nuts and dried figs.
Chlorine	Milk products, cheese, green leafy vegetables, tomatoes, radish, berries, rice, lentils, coconuts and common salt.
Iron	Whole grains, legumes, green vegetables, beets, apricots, raisins, prunes, dates, figs, and nuts.
Magnesium	Wholegrains, green vegetables, apples, alfalfa, soya beans, lemons, peaches, shell fish, dried dates, dried figs, almonds, nuts, pumpkin seeds, sunflower and sesame seeds.
Phosphorous	Milk, curd, cereals, pulses, legumes, pumpkin seeds, fruit juices, and nuts.
Potassium	Milk, cottage cheese, buttermilk, whole grains, lentils, green leafy vegetables, cabbage, celery, broccoli, beetroot, potato, yam, mushroom, tomato, soya bean, guava, custard apple, raspberries, grapes, kiwi fruit, banana, orange, lemon, plum, raisins, dates, figs, apricots, prunes, nuts and pumpkin seeds.
Sodium	Dry lotus stems, leafy vegetables, pulses, legumes, fruits, meat and fish.
Sulphur	Cheese, radish, cabbage, dried beans, eggs and fish.

them. A diet rich in lecithin protects against atherosclerosis.

Vegetable oils, whole grain cereals, peanuts, alfalfa, soyabeans, liver and milk are rich sources of lecithin.

Proteins

Protein is a macronutrient which supplies the body with the essential amino acids. People suffering from heart disease should avoid protein from flesh foods and eggs and instead get their proteins from plant foods. Though flesh foods contain high quality protein they are high in saturated fats and cholesterol and must therefore be avoided.

High Fibre Foods that Protect the Heart

Fibre in g per 100 g of food

Fruits	
Apples	1.42
Bananas	3.40
Oranges	1.90
Pears	2.44
Plums (skin included)	1.52
Strawberries	2.12
Watermelons	1.00
Vegetables	
Beans	2.90
Beetroot	3.10
Brocolli tops	3.60
Brussels sprouts	4.22
Cabbage	3.44
Carrot	2.90
Cauliflower	2.10
Mushrooms	2.50
Okra	3.20
Onions	1.30
Apricot (dried, raw)	24.0
Apricot stewed	8.9
Potatoes	3.41
Radish	1.00
Spinach	6.30
Turnips	2.20
Aubergine	2.5
Legumes and Lentils	
Peas	7.75
Lentils	2.20
Peaches(skin included)	2.28
Cereals and Wheat products	
Oatmeal porridge	7.66
Wheat bran	44.00
Wheat flour (100%)	13.51
White flour	3.45
Nuts	
Almonds	14.30
Coconuts (fresh)	13.60
Peanuts	7.60
Walnuts	5.20
Non-Vegetable foods	
Leak	3.1
Chick Peas	15.0
Sweet Corn (boiled)	4.7
Black currant (raw)	8.7
Dates (dried)	8.7
Figs (dried, raw)	18.5
Prunes (dried raw)	16.1

Dietary Fibre is Important

Fibre is present in the outer layer of seeds, skin of fruits and in vegetables. It cannot be digested by the human body and passes through the digestive tract without being metabolised or broken down. While fibre does not provide any nutrition, it performs other valuable functions; it retains water in the intestine, softens and adds bulk to the stool, prevents constipation, and reduces absorption of dietary cholesterol.

Research has linked high fibre intake with low incidence of heart disease. Communities with low fibre intake have 3 to 4 times more CHD as compared to those with high fibre intake. Medical professionals around the world advocate increasing the fibre intake as an important step in lowering cholesterol and preventing heart disease.

Fibre is of two types: water-soluble and water-insoluble. While water-insoluble fibre is good for digestive disorders and prevents cancer of the colon, water-soluble fibre lowers cholesterol.

The daily consumption of dietary fiber should be 30 to 40g. Overconsumption may be harmful because it interferes with the normal functioning of the digestive system and may cause the loss of valuable nutrients, especially minerals.

Nutrient Supplements : A word of caution

It is best to consult a physician before taking any nutrient or herbal supplements or even nutrient fortified foods because some nutrient and herbal supplements interact adversely with drugs, either by lowering their action or by intensifying or even by producing dangerous side effects.

CHAPTER 7

Foods Good for the Heart

Medical scientists today know more about the influence of diet on heart disease than ever before. Now they know that some components in the food help in reducing the risk of heart disease. These components are found in grains, vegetables and fruits. They are good for the heart, low in calories, high in soluble fibre and reduce blood cholesterol levels.

Cereals

Whole grain cereals such as wheat, maize rice etc. are high in dietary fibre, and good for the heart. They help lower blood cholesterol, are low in fat and high in carbohydrates and proteins. All whole grains and whole grain products have an intrinsic flavour and benefits that are missing from refined grains.

Though grains differ in size, they all have kernels with similar structure. A kernel of grain has three parts: the bran, which is the outer protective covering of the kernel and is a good source of vitamins and fibre; the endosperm which makes up the largest part of the kernel and is a good source of starch and proteins; and the germ, which contains proteins, fat, B-complex vitamins and minerals like iron and phosphorus.

The bran and the germ portions of cereals contain abundant phytochemicals, which are associated with reducing the risk of cardiovascular diseases, diabetes, hypertension, cancer etc. Brown rice, cereal flakes, cereal puffs, whole wheat flour, cracked wheat, rolled oats or oatmeal, and corn meal are made from the entire kernel of the grain.

Bran: Bran is the outer covering (the seed coat) of cereal grains. It is lost in the milling process when the grains are polished and refined. Most B-complex vitamins (riboflavin, niacin, thiamin, pantothenic acid and pyridoxine) reside in bran. Bran is rich in proteins and minerals.

Recently bran has received much attention as a key food in modern living: a rich source of essential fatty acids and essential amino acids. Rice bran, wheat bran and corn bran are rich in insoluble fibres. Oat bran is rich in sticky fibres like mucilage and gum and soluble fibers, which reduce serum cholesterol and blood sugar. It is also an important source of alpha lipoic acid (a micro-nutrient, usually prescribed as a supplement) and coenzyme Q10, which are important oxidants.

Research has shown that a bran diet not only reduces total cholesterol and LDL cholesterol levels, but improves the LDL/HDL ratio. A diet rich in bran helps to reduce weight, relieves constipation, reduces serum cholesterol and blood sugar levels. All cereal brans are available in the form of flour, flakes and tablets. Oats are also available as oatmeal and rolled oats.

It must be remembered, however, that bran should be taken with plenty of fluids to prevent irritation of the gastrointestinal tract.

Brown rice: Brown rice is rich in minerals, protein and fibre. The bran of this unrefined rice is rich in B-complex vitamins. It is a good source of vitamin E.

Cereal puffs: These are as nutritious as the whole grains from which they are made.

Whole Wheat flour: Flour made from whole wheat grain has more nutritional value than white refined flours. If not properly stored, it is subject to rapid deterioration, which is the reason why white (refined) flour is more popular than whole wheat flour. Whole wheat bread is made from the whole wheat flour.

Bulgar Wheat (Lapsi): Wheat that has been soaked, cooked, dried, lightly milled and cracked is known as bulgar wheat. Its nutritive value is similar to that of whole wheat grains. Since it cooks more easily than whole wheat grains, it can be used as a substitute for refined rice.

Wheat germ: The embryo of wheat kernel and a by-product of the wheat milling industry, wheat germ is a good source of vegetable protein, dietary fibres, B-vitamins, vitamin E, minerals and polyunsaturated fatty acids. Research indicates that 30g of wheat germ a day decreases the risks of coronary heart disease by reducing blood cholesterol and blood triglycerides by 10 to 15 per cent. It can also be used as a breakfast cereal, in soups, salads, stews, baked goods, casseroles, and desserts.

Millet: Millet is whole grain with a thick seed coat. It contains better quality protein than rice and wheat but is low in nutrients such as calcium, vitamins A, D, C and B_{12}.

Corn meal: This is produced by grinding the dried (whole) corn kernels. Yellow cornmeal is richer in vitamin A than white cornmeal. It is not only a good source of energy but also contains the antioxidant vitamin E.

Oatmeal: This refers to the commercial 'rolled' oats from which free flour has been removed. The oats are not degerminated. Oatmeal and rolled oats should not be overcooked. Avoid buying oats which do not smell or taste good due to oxidation and rancidity of the germ oil and other components, which accelerate deterioration of the flavour after the cereal has been crushed.

Rye bread: This dark brown bread is made from rye flour and contains more protein, fibre, minerals and B-vitamins than wheat.

Refined cereals like polished rice, refined wheat flour, white bread, biscuits, semolina, vermecelli and noodles should be taken in moderation.

Legumes and Pulses

Legumes and pulses are a rich source of proteins, B-vitamins except B_{12}, and minerals like iron, potassium, phosphorus, magnesium and manganese. They are low in fat and a good alternative to meat for vegetarians. Although legumes and pulses do not contain all essential amino acids, their combination with whole cereal grains and vegetables increases the nutritional value of their protein content. Their fibre content helps in reducing blood sugar and blood cholesterol and prevents constipation.

Sprouts: Sprouts are germinated seeds. Legumes should be sprouted to increase their nutritive value. Sprouted legumes are low in calories and a good source of proteins, fibre, minerals and vitamins.

Alfalfa: Like beans and peas, alfalfa is a legume. Alfalfa sprouts are good for the heart; they are a good source of lecithin, beta carotene, pyridoxine and vitamins C, E and K. Research indicates that alfalfa is an anti-cholesterol agent; it prevents the absorption of dietary cholesterol. Alfalfa can be used as raw salad, vegetable, as a sandwich filling and in soups.

Other wholesome pulses and legumes are sprouted or whole Bengal gram, black gram, cow peas, dry or sprouted, green gram, dry or sprouted, kidney beans or rajmah, and red gram.

Soya: Soya beans are a good source of fat, protein, vitamins and minerals. According to research they are not only an anti-cancer food, but they also protect against cardiovascular disease. Soya protein reduces the total and bad LDL cholesterol by as much as 10 to 20 per cent; it increases HDL cholesterol levels and prevents the formation of plaque in the arteries. It also helps to lower elevated triglyceride levels. It has been found that the omega-3 essential fatty acids present in soya beans improve fat metabolism and cause weight loss.

The isoflavone genistein in soya beans helps to prevent the formation of blood clots as it has antioxidant and anticoagulant properties.

Soya beans should be eaten either as whole beans, soaked, sprouted and made into a gravy, or as flour mixed with whole wheat flour in the ratio of 1:4. Tofu or soya cheese which is high in proteins and B-vitamins can be used in desserts and in savoury dishes. Soya milk makes a good beverage. Defatted soya products are available in the market as soya granules and nuggets.

Meat Analogs

These are vegetarian imitations of meat products made from cereal and legume derivatives like gluten and soy protein. Usually the protein values approximate those of meat, but the level of calories and other nutrients may be quite different. Heart patients should be careful in choosing meat analogs as some of these products are much higher in sodium than fish, meat or poultry.

Nuts

Though nuts are high in calories and fats, heart patients can take moderate amounts of walnuts and Italian chestnuts. The former is the only plant food that provides omega-3 fatty acid, found in fish.

Unsalted Italian chestnuts are lower in fat, protein and calories than almonds, cashew and pistachios. Unlike other nuts, Italian chestnuts are high in complex carbohydrates in the form of starch and fibre. They are best eaten boiled to remove the bitter taste.

Vegetables and Fruits

Wheat grass: Intensive research on the benefits of wheat grass has revealed that wheat grass therapy is an effective remedy for heart diseases, respiratory disease, cancer and the like. Chewing wheat grass or drinking wheat grass juice is an effective remedy for anemia, hypertension, atherosclerosis and thrombosis. Consumption of 100g of wheat grass or 100ml of wheat grass juice everyday proves effective against degenerative diseases.

Citrus fruits: They are rich in vitamin C and phytochemicals, especially carotenoid, the antioxidant that prevents blood clots and protects the heart. They also aid in the absorption of iron in a vegetarian diet.

Apple: Apple fibre helps in reducing total and LDL cholesterol levels in patients with mildly elevated cholesterol. Apples also contain a phytochemical flavonoid quercitin – an antioxidant that inhibits thrombosis.

Pineapple: Fresh pineapple contains bromelain, an enzyme that may help to break up clots.

Other fruits that are beneficial include apricots, black berries, black currants, cherries, dates, grapefruit, grapes, guava which is packed with vitamin C, jack fruit, melons, orange, sweet lime, mango, plum and pomegrenate.

Dried fruits: Though dried fruits like figs, dried apricots, dried prunes, dates and raisins are somewhat higher in calories than their fresh counterparts, they are rich in vitamins and minerals. The soluble fibre reduces total blood cholesterol levels. However, dried fruits should be eaten in moderation and care should be taken that they are free of sulphite compounds.

Herbs and Spices

While many factors influence the types of food we eat, taste dominates in making food choices. That is equally true for a heart patient. Herbs and spices add to taste and flavour, and make food more appetising.

Herbs are fat free and either low in sodium or sodium free. With the exception of celery, which is a source of sodium, herbs are otherwise ideal for people who need to limit their sodium and fat intake. Most herbs like mint, coriander, parsley, basil, sage, oregano, rosemary and cilantro also contain phytochemicals and pigments, which not only have anti-carcinogenic and anti-inflammatory properties but also their antioxidant content protects the heart from the degenarative diseases.

Herbs such as parsley, celery, asparagus and dandelion leaves are natural diuretics (an agent that promotes urine secretion) and help to lower blood pressure by eliminating water and salt from the body. They are also useful in treating heart diseases associated with fluid retention.

Many herbs and spices have both hypoglycemic (blood sugar lowering) and cholesterol reducing properties. They should be included in the daily diet not only to make the food flavoursome, but also for their health benefits.

Turmeric: Turmeric contains a substance called 'curcumin'. A recent experimental study revealed that turmeric reduced cholesterol in animals which had earlier been fed on a high cholesterol diet.

Celery: A compound called 3 n-butyl phthalide found in celery not only acts as a sedative but can also lower blood pressure. Celery helps the kidneys to function efficiently and hastens the excretion of waste from the body. This root vegetable is not only a good source of potassium and vitamin C – important nutrients in the management of heart disease – it also contains soluble fibre which lowers blood cholesterol levels.

Garlic: It has been observed that the daily intake of garlic reduces LDL cholesterol while raising HDL cholesterol. Garlic also retards blood clotting resulting from high fat diet. It inhibits the blood from becoming sticky thus preventing thrombosis. It also decreases blood sugar, lowers blood pressure by dilating blood vessels and helps the blood circulate more freely.

The beneficial effects of garlic are due to its sulphur compounds and essential oils, which have antioxidant properties. Cooking does not decrease its beneficial effects. It is advisable to eat at least 10g of raw garlic a day to protect the body from diabetes and cardiovascular diseases.

Ginger: Ginger contains a number of phenolic compounds which have antioxidant properties. Recent research has shown that ginger can be effective in decreasing serum cholesterol levels and blood pressure.

Onion: Onion protects the body from many degenerative diseases like cardiovascular disease, diabetes and cancer. Like garlic, onion also reverses the adverse effects of a high fat diet. In fact, the blood thinning factor is higher in onion than in garlic. Since onion reduces serum cholesterol and decreases blood sugar by increasing the secretion of insulin, a minimum intake of 100g a day is advisable. Cooking does not alter the activity of this factor.

Ginkgo Biloba: This is a popular Chinese herb and its processed extracts have antioxidant properties. It regulates the tone and elasticity of blood vessels, thereby increasing blood flow. It also helps to reduce the stickiness of the blood, reducing the risk of the formation of blood clots.

Astralagus: The roots of this popular Chinese herb benefit people with heart disease, especially those with the angina (chest pain).

However, it is advisable to consult your doctor before experimenting with Chinese herbs, especially if you are on medication as these herbs may lower the effectiveness of drugs.

Other spices that provide health benefits are caraway, coriander and cumin seeds, and green cardamom and asafoetidoa. However, spices like red and green chillis, cloves, cinnamon, black cardamom, mace, mango powder, nutmeg, pepper, poppy seeds and tamarind should be taken in moderation.

Seeds

Flax seeds: These are a good source of omega-3 fatty acids. They are useful in treating blood pressure, angina and in lowering cholesterol levels.

Watermelon seeds: Watermelon seeds help in reducing blood pressure.

Fenugreek seeds: These seeds are a rich source of soluble fibre. In addition, they contain an alkaloid known to reduce blood sugar levels. They also lower serum cholesterol and triglycerides and offer protection from degenerative diseases like diabetes and coronary heart problems.

For chronic diabetics, a daily intake of 25g of fenugreek seed powder in two doses is essential. Others should make it a habit to take 1 to 2 teaspoons fenugreek seed powder every day.

Milk and Milk Producs

Milk is a source of lactose sugar, a complete protein because it contains all the essential amino acids. Low fat or skimmed milk has about 75% fewer calories and about 80% less fat than buffalo milk. Cow's milk is also low in fat and calories and preferable to buffalo milk. Milk is a good source of vitamin A, the B vitamins thiamin, riboflavin, niacin and especially cobalamin, and vitamin D. Calcium and phosphorus are the main minerals found in milk.

Curd: Curd, or yogurt, is fermented milk and is nature's way of making food more easily digestible and palatable. It should be prepared from low fat cow milk or skimmed milk. Curd neutralises the excess acid in the stomach, and plays a vital role in cleansing out the toxic putrefying matter from the body. A nutritious food, curd prevents constipation and aids digestion.

Yogurt with acidophilus bacteria culture: This commercial yogurt available in some countries is prepared with the friendly bacteria acidophilus and not the usual bifidus culture. Research indicates that this health promoting bacteria tends to absorb the cholesterol in the intestine before it can reach the arteries and cause damage.

Honey

Though honey is a source of calories, it is an excellent remedy for obesity because it mobilises the extra fat deposited in the body and puts it into circulation, which is then utilised as energy for normal function. Honey also acts as a mild laxative and prevents constipation. When taken regularly, aids in digestion and prevents discomfort after meals.

Honey protects against chest congestion, colds and sore throats. Apart from being the source of sugar and energy, it also contains vitamins B_2, B_6, C, H and K, as well as a number of trace elements. Honey is an important source of 'ferments', which are biologically active protective substances valuable for the proper functioning of the heart. Honey should be used instead of refined sugar, raw sugar or jaggery in juices and desserts.

Other Foods Good for the Heart

Organic foods: These are foods that have been grown in soil enriched with organic rather than chemical fertilizers and without the use of pesticides. Organically processed foods are not treated with preservatives, horomones, antibiotic or synthetic additives. They are safe to eat because they have a longer shelf life and retain some nutrients which are lost in conventionally grown foods. Moreover, organically processed foods contain some trace elements absorbed from the soil, which are usually not present in the conventionally grown and processed foods.

Coconut water: Coconut water is a cooling drink and helps to flush out crystals of calcium, phosphorus and urea salts from the system through the urine.

Barley water: This is also a cooling drink and helps to remove excess water from the body during oedema. Barley water also helps to flush out calcium, potassium and urea salts through the urine.

Green tea: People who consume green tea every day are at a lower risk of heart diseases. Green tea protects against heart diseases because the polyphenols in it, are a powerful antioxidant. They prevent damage to LDL cholesterol thereby preventing the build-up of plaque in the arteries.

Red wine: Red wine is derived during fermentation from the natural pigment present in the skin of dark coloured grapes. The phenolic compounds of red grapes and of red wine have been shown to reduce the bad LDL cholesterol levels and the ethyl alcohol content of red wine raises the good HDL cholesterol. The phenolic flavonoids present in red wine inhibit thrombosis and protect against heart diseases. These chemicals also cause the excretion of bile acid and fat.

Since it is the ethyl alcohol content that increases HDL cholesterol levels, red wine taken in moderation is not harmful. Taken in excess, alcohol adds extra calories and contributes to other health.

Pectin: A dry powder of a carbohydrate gum used to make gels, pectin does not have any nutritional value and is a popular anti-diarrhoea remedy. Medicinally it is used to lower blood cholesterol. Citrus pectin appears to be much more effective than apple pectin in lowering cholesterol.

Psyllium seeds: Available as ground refined or unrefined seeds in granule or powder form, these psyllium seeds do not have any nutritional value but are a source of dietary fibre and used as a laxative. Psyllium helps to lower cholesterol by binding cholesterol to the bile in the digestive tract, causing the body to draw cholesterol from the bloodstream. Refined psyllium products are recommended for heart patients with irritated bowels.

CHAPTER 8

Foods Bad for the Heart

Use them with care!

Many ready-to-eat, packaged and convenience foods available today have either lost their essential nutrients during processing or contain additives in the form of colour, flavour enhancers, excess fat, salt and sugar, all of which can cause degenerative ailments, especially cardiovascular diseases. These and certain foods that harm the heart should be avoided or taken in limited quantities.

Sodium

Salt, or sodium chloride, is an essential part of our diet. It not only adds flavour and taste to food, but also assists in maintaining the balance of body fluids. Table salt is the most obvious source of sodium (it is 40 per cent sodium and 60 per cent chloride). However, increasingly the sodium that is added to processed foods or ready-to-eat convenience foods is becoming the greatest contributor to the total amount of sodium consumed. In addition many natural sources of food like meat, milk and vegetables also contain sodium.

Adults do not require more than 3 to 7g of salt per day in cold climates. In hot, humid conditions 8 to 10g of salt is not harmful. Each gram of salt contains 400mg of sodium; a teaspoon of salt provides 2g of sodium.

The natural sodium content of foods: Natural sodium, as distinct from chemical sodium, is found in almost all foods that we eat. Animal foods have a relatively higher sodium content than plant foods. Meat, poultry, eggs, milk and cheese are high in sodium content. Organ meats such as brain, liver and kidney contain more sodium than the muscle meats. Amongst fish, shell fish such as prawn, lobster, crab, squid and mussels have higher sodium content than other fishes. Even some plant foods like spinach, carrot and beans contain significant amount of sodium.

Fruits, most vegetables and cereals contain insignificant amount of sodium. Drinking water may sometimes contain appreciable quantities of sodium. Water softeners raise the sodium content of water.

Other sources of sodium: Sodium, in combination with a number of chemicals other than chloride, is used in many processed foods. Such foods are best avoided. It is found in vegetable salt which is used as seasoning, in baking soda (sodium bicarbonate) and baking powder.

Monosodium glutamate (MSG), is a flavour enhancer used in Chinese cuisine, in baked products, quick cooking cereals and in brine (salt water) used to preserve meat and fish. It is used as an additive in ice-creams and other frozen products, in chocolate drinks, jams, jellies and desserts, and to soften hard water.

Foods that are high in saturated fat, hydrogenated fat and foods rich in cholesterol have high sodium content.

Why is Excess Salt Harmful?

Any excess sodium consumed through salt and other foods is retained in the body and this can accelerate major heart disease risk factors such as diabetes, hypertension and hyperlipidaemia. It also causes water retention leading to oedema. Salt consumption of 10 to 20g or more a day can lead to stroke and heart diseases.

Not Salt, but Sodium, is the Culprit

There is often a confusion in understanding the difference between the terms 'sodium restricted diet' and 'salt restricted diet'. In fact, the diet should be sodium restricted and not salt restricted. It is the sodium, and not the chloride, that is potentially harmful to the heart.

Even for a healthy person it is safe to limit the intake of sodium as a part of healthier diet, more so as one grows older. This reduces the risk of coronary heart disease and high blood pressure.

Are Low Sodium Foods Really Low in Sodium?

Low-sodium foods are used when a person requires sodium-restricted diet. Such foods should contain no more than 120mg of sodium per 100g of the final product. Very low-sodium foods should contain 40mg of sodium per 100g.

However, many so-called low sodium foods available commercially may not really be low in sodium. The preservatives and salt substitutes added to increase the flavour actually increase the sodium content of these foods. Low sodium foods should be consumed only if the manufacturer has removed sodium from the food, not added sodium based preservatives or salt substitutes and enhanced the flavour with herbs and spices.

If low sodium foods are actually low in sodium, their long term use is beneficial.

Confusion also arises from the terms salt-free or 'free from added salt'. In fact, these foods actually contain a considerable amount of salt and may harm people with heart problems who need to control their sodium intake.

Foods That Raise Cholesterol

People with heart problems and those who have a family history of heart disease or high blood cholesterol should limit dietary cholesterol. In fact, even healthy people should stay away from cholesterol-rich foods to prevent obesity, hypertension, coronary heart diseases and diabetes mellitus.

There are certain foods like pies, biscuits, cakes, chocolates, pastries, dairy products — butter, cheese, cream, ghee, hydrogenated ghee — margarine, coconut oil and coffee which, whether taken in moderation or in excess are harmful for the heart. Their intake should be limited or avoided.

Red meats: Red meat is definitely not for those suffering from heart problems. Though a good source of proteins and vitamins, it is full of saturated fat. All flesh foods leave a highly acidic ash and may lead to acidosis which aggravates the health of those already suffering from heart disease.

Flesh foods also take a long time to be digested and overload the bowel with toxic putrefying matter which can cause discomfort and strain the heart.

For die-hard meat-eaters, chicken, with the fat and skin removed, is a good alternative. It may be added to the diet: about 50g per serving, once or twice a week.

Shell fish: Although fish are an excellent alternative to animal meat and are generally good for the heart, one needs to be selective in the case of shell fish. Some may be consumed; others avoided. Shell fish, especially shrimps, prawns, lobsters and squids are high in dietary cholesterol and should be avoided.

Eggs: It is best to limit intake of eggs to one or two per week. The egg yolk is rich in cholesterol, and contains 200 to 300mg of cholesterol. But the white of the egg contains albumin, and is cholesterol free.

Processed Foods

Most processed foods have their nutrients damaged or destroyed either by the heating or chemical processing involved. The molecules of the damaged nutrients are no longer useful and interfere with the functioning of the nervous system. Additionally, the body has to cope with their excretory burden.

Preserved meats and fish: Salted meat and fish not only contain excess salt, but also chemical additives. They are often packed in brine; sometimes even crude salt or sea salt is used. Chemical agents like monosodium glutamate or monopotassium glutamate are used to enhance flavour. Processed meats such as sausage, bacon and ham are also preserved as smoked products with nitrites used as preservatives. Nitrites convert to nitrosamines, a potentially carcinogenic substance formed in the food or in the stomach when the nitrites react with the amines.

Convenience foods: Some convenience foods such as fat-free cookies, fat-free cream, cheese, baked chips etc., in fact contain substances that can raise triglyceride levels.

Refined cereals: Cereals that have had the bran and the germ removed from the kernel during processing contain only starch. These refined cereals are devoid of minerals, vitamins and fibre, and provide only energy and incomplete protein. These are rapidly absorbed by the body and increase blood sugar levels, causing the pancreas to secrete more insulin to bring the sugar levels down. This ultimately leads to insulin resistance, excess weight and adult diabetes, which in turn reduces blood circulation and cause heart diseases.

Sugar: Both white and brown sugar (also called raw sugar) are the same in composition and nutritional value and provide only calories. Sugar is best avoided or taken in very small quantities.

Baked foods: Since salt is added to the raw flour while making bread, the end product is rich in sodium. Baking soda and baking powder, both of which are high in sodium, are used in cookies, biscuits, pies, cakes, etc. Baked foods also sometimes contain additives which are high in sodium. In addition, most baked foods use plastic shortening, or margarine (similar to dairy butter in composition) or butter as a fat source which are rich in saturated fats and in cholesterol.

Regular intake of refined flours, sugar packed foods, sweets, fluffy breads and chips often results in a person becoming sluggish, jittery and irritable. These simple carbohydrate foods cause a steep rise and fall in blood sugar levels, and lead to obesity and type 2 diabetes, all of which are risk factors for cardiovascular diseases.

Icecream, jams, jellies and chocolate: Generally these are high in sugar content, calories, saturated fats and cholesterol. They contain additives such as emulsifiers, stabilizers and thickeners.

Low fat spreads or very low fat spreads: Though low fat spreads and very low fat spreads are low in fat (40g and 25g of fat per 100g respectively) as compared to oils and butter margarine, they are still a dietary risk factor because of a much higher salt content.

Soups, sauces and salad dressings: Ready to drink or pre-cooked soups contain monosodium glutamate as well as emulsifiers and thickeners. All these are high in sodium content. So are most sauces, specially soya sauce.

Fatty Acid Composition and Cholesterol Content of Animal Foods (g/100g edible portion)

Foods	Fat Content	Saturated	Cholesterol*
Buffalo's milk	6.5	4.0	16
Cheese	24.1	15.0	100
Chicken with skin	18.0	6.0	100
Chicken without skin	4.0	1.0	60
Condensed milk (canned)	10.0	6.0	40
Cow's milk	4.0	2.0	14
Cream	13.0	8.0	40
Curd (from whole milk)	6.5	6.0	16
Egg (whole)	13.3	4.0	400
Egg yolk	30.0	9.0	1120
Evaporated milk (whole milk)	7.5	5.0	30
Mutton	13.0	7.0	65
Skimmed milk	0.1	-	2
Organ Meats			
Brain	6.0	2.0	2000
Heart	5.0	2.0	150
Kidney	2.0	1.0	370
Liver	9.0	3.0	300
Fresh Water and Sea Foods			
Clams	1.2	0.35	51
Crab	2.2	0.37	100
Fish (lean)	1.5	0.4	45
Fish (fatty)	6.0	2.5	45
Oysters	1.7	0.58	50
Prawns/shrimps	2.0	0.3	150

*Values in milligram (mg) per 100 gram(g).

Fatty Acid Composition and Cholesterol Content of Popular Foods

Foods*	Fat	Saturated	Cholesterol	Cal**
1 cheese burger (112g)	15	7.3	44	300
1 chicken frankfurter (45g)	9	2.5	45	115
1 chicken patti (60)	12	3	40	180
1 croissant (58g)	12	3.5	13	235
1 cup cake (35g)	4	1.8	19	120
1 cup egg noodles (160g)	2	0.5	50	200
1 cup rich custard (148g)	24	14.7	88	350
1 cup spaghetti with meat balls & tomato sauce (250g)	12	5.9	89	330
1 cup Vanilla icecream (133g)	14	8.9	58	270
1 doughnut (50g)	12	2.8	20	210
1 fish and cheese sandwich(140g)	23	6.3	56	420
1 muffin (45g)	5	1.5	19	135
1 nut cookie (25g)	4	1.6	14	100
1 piece apple pie (150g)	18	4.6	0	405
1 piece cheese cake (90g)	18	9.9	170	280
1 piece lemon meringue (140g)	14	4.3	143	355
1 slice cake (70g)	8	3	36	235
1 slice cheese pizza (120g)	9	4.1	56	290
1 slice French toast (65g)	7	1.6	112	155
1 waffle (75g)	13	4.0	102	245
Egg Preparations				
1 egg, fried in butter	7	2.7	278	95
1 egg, poached	6	1.7	273	80
1 egg, scrambled	8	3.2	282	110
Salad Dressings				
1 tbsp mayonnaise (15g)	11	1.7	8	100
1 tbsp thousand island dressing (15g)	6	1.0	4	60
1 tbsp French dressing (15g)	9	1.4	0	85

*Values in milligram (mg) per 100 gram(g).
**Calories in kilo calories

Most salad dressings contain 35 to 50 per cent oil, a starch paste as thickner and egg yolk. It is best to keep such dressings away or use them minimally.

Fried Foods/Fast Foods

Commercially produced fried foods are generally made in saturated fat especially hydrogenated fat and oil, which are often used and reused several times resulting in the formation of free radicals. These free radicals affect the blood vessels and the heart and are also carcinogenic.

Fast foods such as French fries, burgers, pizzas, kababs and other deep fried foods, as well as shakes and colas are high in saturated fats and calories. They are also high in salt and low in fibre.

Raw, Whole Milk and Dairy Products

Unpasteurized milk can be a source of two dreaded diseases – brucellosis and tuberculosis. Even pasteurized milk should be limited in a sodium restricted diet, because of its high sodium content. Avoid whole milk and dairy products because they are high in saturated fats.

CHAPTER 9

The Healing Diets

There is no doubt that the right foods provide dramatic protection and keep heart disease at bay. A well-balanced diet provides all nutrients required for a healthy heart. In fact diet is now considered as an alternative to drugs and surgery; the mantra for healthy and disease free living.

The correct selection of foods also plays an important role in management, treatment and recovery from heart disease.

The primary objectives in regulating the diet of heart patients is to provide maximum rest for the heart, to reduce weight in the obese, and to prevent illness.

Changes in the diet, if sustained, can and do reduce the risk of further heart disease. However, these changes need adequate psychological, family and social support to convert these into permanent dietary habits.

The dietary guidelines for different heart diseases are just that: guidelines. They are given only to facilitate understanding. Individual patients have to be treated based on the state of their health, weight, height and any complications, such as diabetes, hypertension, etc. For example, the diet for a heart patient with ideal body weight will be different from the one who is an obese.

Dietary Guidelines for Coronary Heart Disease

The aim of the diet is to reduce the lipid levels by reducing both dietary saturated fatty acids and dietary cholesterol. The dietary goals of treatment are to maintain appropriate body weight and normal blood pressure, to regulate the blood lipids, glucose and insulin levels, to prevent the aggregation of some blood factors like platelets and fibrin, and to increase the antioxidant levels in the body.

Calories: The calorie intake should be just enough to meet the daily requirements. Excessive intake of calories will cause elevation of blood cholesterol and other lipids in the plasma.

Carbohydrates: Carbohydrates in the diet should consist mostly of starch. Too much carbohydrate should be avoided because it is converted into fat, which then raises cholesterol and triglyceride levels. Glucose and sucrose should be reduced because they too increase blood cholesterol.

Tips for a Healthy Diet

- Small meals are preferable to large, bulky meals. Large meals tend to burden the digestive system and the heart.
- Soft bland diets with easy-to-chew and easy-to-digest foods are advised.
- Complex carbohydrates and products with complex carbohydrates should be preferred over refined carbohydrates like white flour and sugar.
- Excess protein should be avoided.
- Saturated and hydrogenated fats should be avoided. Polyunsaturated oils like sunflower, soya bean, and monounsaturated oils like canola and olive oil used.
- Avoid foods rich in saturated fat and dietary cholesterol.
- Sugar intake should be minimal and foods containing sugar avoided.
- Salt intake should be restricted to no more than 3g per day.
- High fibre diet with adequate fluid intake is essential to avoid constipation.
- Dietary fibre intake of about 30g per day is recommended.
- Vitamin or nutrition supplements should always be taken under medical advise.

Proteins: Protein intake should be normal, unless the patient is obese and has been advised to lose weight. Protein too is converted to fat in the body, raising cholesterol and triglycerides. Non-vegetarians can get their protein from fish and small amounts of chicken, with the skin and fat removed, taken once or twice a week. Vegetarians get their proteins from legumes and pulses.

Egg whites are allowed as they do not contain any cholesterol at all.

Milk and milk products: Non-fat skimmed milk or very low fat milk and curd prepared from it, and 3 to 4 tablespoons of very low fat cheese or tofu without salt can be added to the diet.

Vitamins and minerals: The vitamin and mineral intake should meet the daily requirements. Vitamin C is especially necessary for capillary stability. Niacin (B_3) and B-vitamins reduce blood lipid levels. Adequate, but not excess, amounts of potassium and calcium in the blood are required to prevent arrhythmias.

Vegetables and fruit: Fruits and vegetables are a good source of vitamins, minerals and antioxidants. A few servings of vegetables and fruits every day lower the risk of coronary heart disease by 20 per cent. Each additional serving cuts the risk by another 20 per cent. The protective effect is less among the overweight and/or those who smoke.

Onion and garlic should be included in the daily diet since they possess anti-platelet aggregation property.

Salt: Dietary salt should be reduced as much as possible. Not more than 500mg to 1000mg a day is recommended. However, if more than this amount is taken, then the intake of potassium rich foods, such as fruits, should be increased to balance the sodium intake.

Dietary Guidelines for Hyperlipidemias

Since people with hyperlipidemias suffer from increased serum lipid levels, the aim of the diet is to reduce the lipid levels. To achieve this, a diet that is restricted in cholesterol and saturated fatty acid is recommended.

Calories: In overweight and obese persons the calories are reduced to achieve weight reduction, otherwise the calorie intake should be just adequate to maintain ideal body weight.

Fats and oils: Saturated and hydrogenated fats which increase cholesterol levels should be avoided, as also fried foods. All foods that increase cholesterol levels, such as egg (yolk), red meats, baked foods, should be avoided. Alcohol should also be avoided.

Carbs: Complex carbohydrates and the products made with them should be preferred. However, even complex carbohydrates should be taken in moderation as they also convert to fat and increase lipid levels.

Dietary Guidelines for Arrhythmias

Oily fish like sardines, salmon, tuna, mackerel etc. may be taken 3 to 4 times a week, (but not if these are canned in oil or salt water). Include foods that are rich in magnesium, potassium, manganese and coenzyme Q-10. Avoid caffeine-rich beverages, alcohol and smoking. Follow the dietary guidelines for other heart diseases.

Dietary Guidelines for Congestive Heart Failure

Diet is very important in the management of congestive cardiac failure. The diet should be easily digestible; mini meals are recommended. Since the patient is at rest, the calorie requirement is slightly less than that of a sedentary adult. Carbohydrates should form the main bulk of the diet. Protein intake should be minimum since kidney impairment is a symptom of congestive heart failure.

Fats and oils: Fat intake should be low because of liver enlargement. Saturated fats, hydrogenated fats, cholesterol rich foods and all fried foods must be avoided. Palatability of food should be increased with herbs and mild spices.

Salt: Since patients suffering from congestive heart failure suffer from breathlessness, oedma, enlargement of the liver and impaired renal function, a sodium restricted or low sodium diet is recommended. Depending upon the severity of the condition, the daily intake of sodium should not be more than 200 to 400mg. Cooking, as far as possible, should be salt free. All processed foods should be avoided. Only foods that contain natural sodium are permitted so that the daily intake of sodium maintains the acid-base balance of the blood.

The diet should contain potassium rich foods or supplemented with potassium salts, as advised by doctor, to make up for the loss of potassium salts in the urine since diuretics are administered to reduce oedema. Fluid restriction should be proportional to the degree of congestive cardiac failure. In other words, the degree to which sodium, and sometimes fluids, are restricted depends on the needs of the individual.

Dieticians have to be very cautious while prescribing a low sodium diet. There is always a danger of depleting the body of sodium. Sodium depletion may cause weakness abdominal cramps, lethargy and disturbance in the acid-base balance.

Dietary Guidelines for Myocardial Infarction

People suffering from myocardial infarction are recommended a liquid diet. Since myocardial infarction is accompanied by cardiac dysfunction and fall in blood pressure, the diet should be modified depending upon the severity of the condition.

For the first three days the patient should be on a clear liquid diet consisting of 1 to 15 litres of strained fruit juice, strained vegetable juice, tea with sugar, coconut water, barley water containing glucose, and glucose water.

This should be followed by a full liquid diet for three days which should include milk or a cereal or a dal soup. A full cup of this liquid diet is necessary at an interval of 3 to 4 hours. The daily full fluid diet requirement is around 1 litre. This diet provides the minimum requirements of proteins, vitamins and minerals.

For the next three days, a semi liquid easily digestable diet like pudding or a porridge providing approximately 1000kcal a day is suggested.

Following the semi liquid diet, three days of a soft solid diet that includes *khichdi, idli,* curd, rice, soft dal, tender boiled vegetables providing 1200kcal a day is recommended. The diet should be low in calories, fat and sodium and have zero cholesterol.

The diet should not include excess fibre, spices and condiments. However, herbs can be used to enhance the flavour and to prevent flatulence and aid digestion.

Dietary Guidelines for Heart Disease with Hypertension

The diet for a hypertension patient should include just enough calories to meet the daily requirement.

Salt: Depending upon the severity of the hypertension, salt intake should be restricted or low. However, all foods that contain sodium should be avoided.

Fats and oils: Foods rich in saturated and hydrogenated fats and cholesterol should be avoided. They are high both in fats and sodium. Processed and refined foods, percolated and brewed coffee and soft drinks are harmful for hypertensives.

Other foods: The diet should include complex carbohydrates, and should be high in fibre. It should include foods that are rich in antioxidants, reduce cholesterol and increase diuretic activity. Natural foods which reduce hypertension are onion, garlic, ginger, basil, parsley, celery, asparagus, wheat grass, citrus fruits, oat bran and natural products like pectin and psyllium seeds which contain soluble fibre are known to reduce hypertension. Weight reduction, giving up smoking and alcohol, regular exercise like brisk walking, yoga and relaxation also help to reduce hypertension.

Dietary Guidelines for Heart Disease with Stress

The diet should consist of plenty of foods that are rich in antioxidants to neutralise the free radical load. The diet should also include foods that contain the essential vitamins and minerals that act as anti-stress nutrients.

Whole grain cereals, a variety of legumes, fruits, vegetables, and fish supply the necessary complex carbohydrates, while plant proteins provide the essential amino acids and PUFA fats provide the essential fatty acids.

Dietary Guidelines for Heart Disease with Diabetes

Heart patients with maturity on-set diabetes should control the disease not only with the anti-diabetic medication but also with diet.

Sugars: The diet should be free of refined sugar, honey, and jaggery. In other words, foods with a high glycemia index should be avoided. Cereals, and more so refined cereals, sugars and root tubers have a high glycemia index. Fruits have an intermediate glycemia index. Legumes have a low glycemia index, vegetables (not including tubers) have the least.

Other foods: The diet should be slightly low in carbohydrates and fats. Saturated and hydrogenated fats and foods rich in cholesterol should

Glycaemic Index of Selected Foods

Foods with low glycaemic index increase blood sugar slowly and are better for diabetics than diets with high glycaemic index.

Low Glycaemic Foods 10%-39%	soyabeans, groundnuts, kidney beans, all lentils, legumes, vegetables chick peas, apple, skimmed milk, curd, yogurt, ice cream.
Intermediate Glycaemic Foods 40%-69%	fruits, whole meals, beans, sweet potato, peas, Bengal gram, corn, bread, rice (brown), shredded wheat, beetroot, raisins.
High Glycaemic Foods 70%-100%	cereals (refined), root tubers, millets, rice (white) broad beans, corn flakes, carrot, honey, potato mashed.

be totally avoided. These also include fruits like custard apple, sapota, dried fruits and nuts. A diet rich in fibre, especially soluble fibre which reduces blood sugar levels, is recommended.

Powdered fenugreek seeds added to buttermilk or to other foods help to reduce blood sugar, as does exercise and abstaining from alcohol.

Dietary Guidelines for Heart Dieases for the Overweight or Obese

Reducing body weight and bringing it down within the recommended range is the primary objective of dietary management of obese heart patients. Weight reduction lowers the risk of cardio-vascular disease. It leads to reduced levels of cholesterol and triglycerides, as also lowering of blood pressure and blood sugar.

Calories: A low calorie diet that provides fewer calories than the total energy requirement for the day is recommended. This diet should not have more than 1200 to 1300kcal/day. It should be low in fats but high in complex carbohydrates. Proteins should be derived from cereals and legumes which are low in calories. Very low calorie diets are nutritionally not balanced and extremely harmful. These should be avoided.

Most obese people have low basal metabolic rates and hence low energy expenditure. So modified diets should be combined with regular aerobic exercise (brisk walking) to increase the metabolism and the expenditure of energy.

A balance between energy intake and energy expenditure will help to maintain the ideal body weight.

CHAPTER 10

Towards a Healthier Life

Lifestyle adjustments are very important for managing, treating and preventing heart disease. This essentially requires developing a healthier diet pattern and a more physically active daily routine.

You are What You Eat

Leading health experts agree that sensible eating habits are the way to health, energy and vitality. A recent study in UK revealed that 80 per cent of cardiovascular disease may have been related to diet. Similarly American Heart Association advises that dietary changes must be made to reduce the risk of heart disease. Diet is implicated in two major factors leading to it – high blood pressure and high blood cholesterol levels.

Eat right : Making permanent changes in your eating habits is the key to good health. Not 'going on a diet', but healthy eating is the answer. Healthy eating based on sound nutrition is the long term strategy to good health, good looks and feeling great.

People with heart disease should drink breakfast, that is, have a nutritious beverage for breakfast, followed by a moderate lunch and a light dinner at least two hours before going to bed.

Count your calories: Modify your favourite dishes to lower their fat content and not their taste.

Reduce salt and sugar: Use herbs and spices instead of salt. Replace refined sugars with fruit sugars.

Avoid heavy meals: Heavy meals can put a load on the heart and slow down the digestive process causing discomfort.

Be a vegetarian: Vegetarian diets are low in fat, especially saturated fat, and contain zero cholesterol. Vegetarians also tend to have a lower body mass index.

Add fibre to your diet: An easy way to add fibre to your food without changing its taste is to sprinkle it with cereal bran.

Healthy Snacking: Snacking, if it is of the right type, can keep the body energised through the day and prevents overeating at meal times.

The Food Pyramid*

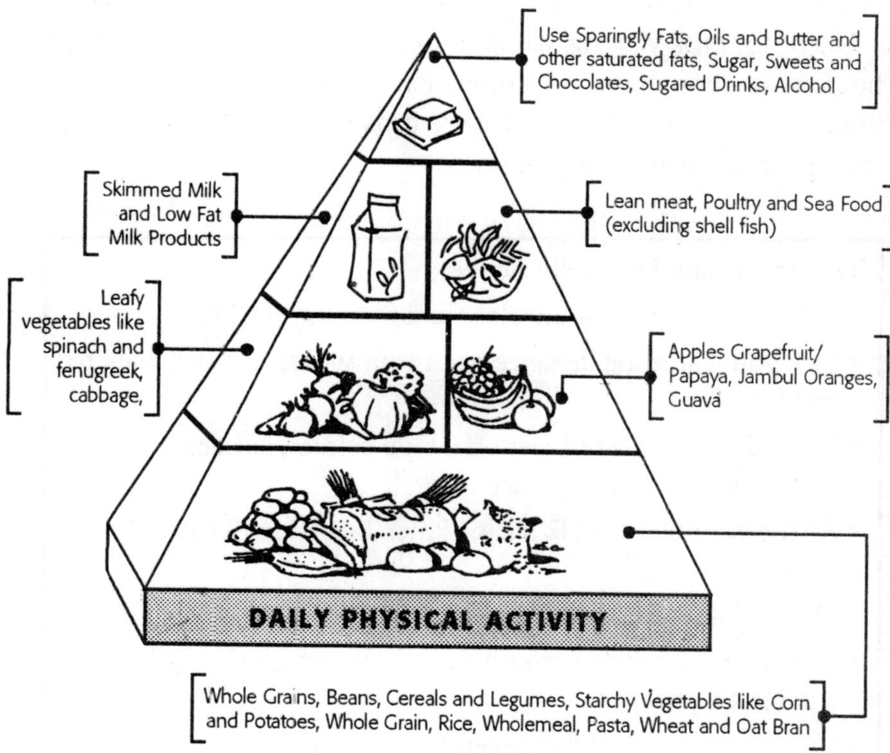

* Adapted from the Food Pyramid of the American Heart Association.

Replace Fried Snacks: Fresh fruit and sliced vegetables with low calorie homemade dips make an excellent snack.

Eat More Fruit: Unless diabetic, even a heart patient can enjoy 4-5 servings of fresh fruit at any time. Fruits are low in calories and high in minerals, vitamins and fibre.

Fit Forever

Exercise is an important health habit. It has significant positive impact both on preventing and on speeding up recovery from cardiovascular disease. Regular physical activity not only reduces the chances of heart attack but the effect of heart disease is also much less severe on a person who exercises regularly. The health benefits of exercise unfortunately cannot be stored. Once developed, to retain the benefits of exercise, the habit has to be maintained lifelong, year-after-year.

Except for brisk walking, all other exercises including yoga, should be done under professional supervision. It is absolutely essential for those with a history of heart disease to consult their cardiologist before starting on an exercise programme.

TIPS to Remain Physically Active

- Take the staircase for one floor and then use the lift.
- Park your car some distance from your workplace and walk to and fro.
- If you are taking a bus, get off a stop before your destination and then walk that distance.
- At the workplace, walk during lunch break for 10 to 15 minutes.
- Do mild household chores as an exercise.
- If you have a pet dog, take it for a walk, which should become a daily routine.
- Gardening is a good daily exercise.
- Plan an after dinner walk with someone.

Exercise Guidelines

Regular moderate activity is more protective and beneficial than small amounts of heavy activity.

Begin slowly: Begin slowly with a 10-minute walk, twice or thrice a week.

Frequency: Exercise at least 3 to 4 times a week.

Duration: Should not exceed 20 to 30 minutes.

Intensity: The intensity of the exercise should be within the patient's target heart rate zone rather than below or above it.

Weather check: Avoid exercising if the temperature and humidity are too high or too low. It can be harmful. In summer, exercise during the cool hours of early morning or late evening. During winter months, exercise indoors.

Clothing: Wear light, loose cotton clothes in summer. Wear several layers of clothes during winter.

Timing: Exercise at least two hours before or after meals. Never immediately after meals.

Warm up session: Always begin with a 5-minute warm up session to prepare the body, muscles and joints for stress of exercise.

Cool down session: This should be the concluding 5 minutes of the exercise routine to let the body come to its normal state.

Listen to your body: If there is any discomfort such as difficulty in breathing, nausea, feeling of weakness, sweating, chest pain for over a long time, discontinue exercising and consult your physician immediately.

Yoga

Regular practice of yoga can prevent the reoccurrence of heart and hypertension problems and the ill effects of sedentary lifestyle. Yoga asanas and pranayama help in lowering blood pressure, in minimising the effect of diabetes as a risk factor and in controlling atherosclerosis and angina. Yoga is also a great stress buster.

Recent studies by the All India Institute of Medical Sciences, New Delhi, indicate that yoga asanas, along with dietary modifications resulted in positive changes in the overall health of heart patients. It was found that the benefits become apparent within seven days of starting the yoga programme.

If you are stressed and physically inactive, re-evaluate your stressors, current work and leisure time and change to a more active lifestyle with regular exercise and yoga.

Delicious Choices

Eating for a healthy heart

Some Healthy Cooking Tips

Vegetable Stock for Soups

All soups start with stock or liquids. Making soup stock is economical, nutritious and delicious. To prepare vegetable stock boil vegetables (carrot, tomatoes, cauliflower, cabbage, or any vegetables of your choice) in water with parsley, mint, basil, coriander leaves and cloves, black and green cardamoms, cinnamon sticks. Cook on a slow fire for 10-15 minutes and strain. Use this vegetable liquid or stock to prepare soups.

Nutritious Sprouts

To sprout beans and legumes, clean and soak them overnight in filtered water. Drain and spread it on a sieve or strainer, cover with a plate or cloth, place on a stand and leave in a warm, dark place for two days. Alternatively, tie the drained beans in muslin and hang for two days, till the translucent, white shoots are 1 to 2 cm long. Remember to sprinkle water 2-3 times a day during the germinating process.

Sprouts have enormous health benefits, add zest to a salad or can be a replacement to your salad.

Fresh sprouts are not only delicious, but full of bioactive vitamins, minerals, enzymes and amino acids. Vitamins in sprouts remain intact. Enzymes in sprouts increase the body's ability to digest nutrients. Sprouts provide all necessary amino acids for the body and contain no saturated fat or cholesterol.

Curry Powder

Curry powder is a ready-to-use ground mixture of spices and herbs which eliminates the inconvenience of using individual spices which maybe required in a recipe. It is used in dishes which need subtle curry flavours; it is neither highly aromatic and nor does it dominate or mash other flavours. It is easily prepared at home.

2 tsp Bengal gram
4 tsp corinader seeds
½ tsp cumin seeds
¼ tsp fenugreek seeds
¼ tsp pepper seeds
3 red chillies

Roast the ingredients lightly and grind them to a powder. Store in airtight glass container for future use.

Soups & Salads

About Soups and Salads

- Soups are filling as well as nutritious. They are a good source of minerals and vitamins.
- Clear vegetable soups are preferable to cream based soups and soups made with red meat or with dollops of butter added.
- Never strain soups after liquidizing the vegetables and fruits. Fibre will be lost if you do.
- Soups maybe served hot in winter and cold, not chilled, in summer.
- Use home-made vegetable stock to prepare soups. Boil vegetables with herbs and spices. Cook on a slow fire for 10-15 minutes and strain to get a nutritious soup stock.
- Salads are crisp and filling.
- They are rich in fibre, and add bulk to the diet.
- Salads made with a combination of sprouts, vegetables and fruits are wholesome and nutritious.
- Avoid high calorie, high fat salad dressings like French, thousand island, vinaigrette and mayonnaise.
- Use citrus fruit juice with a dash of mild spices or curd and a variety of chopped herbs to make salad dressing.

Healthy Vegetable Soup

Nutrition Facts

Calories	167.0 kcal
Carbs	35.7g
Fat	0.61g
Fibre	4.0g
Minerals	2.2g
Protein	6.1g

½ cup cooked rice
2 onions, peeled and chopped
1 carrot, peeled and diced
½ cup peas, shelled
½ cup cauliflower florets
½ litre water
½ tsp ginger-garlic paste
A handful of French beans, chopped
A pinch of pepper powder
A pinch of cumin powder
A pinch of salt

Garnish

1 tbsp celery leaves, chopped

Bring the water to a boil and add the vegetables. Add the remaining ingredients when the vegetables are tender. Mix well, cover the vessel, and let simmer for 10 minutes over low heat.

Serve hot, without straining, garnished with chopped celery leaves.

Makes 2 servings

Sprouty Soup

Nutrition Facts

Calories	80.0 kcal
Carbs	8.0g
Fat	3.5g
Fibre	0.65g
Minerals	0.64g
Protein	3.9g

1 cup mixed sprouts (whole green gram, & Bengal gram, soya beans & kidney beans)

½ litre water

½ tsp cumin and pepper powder

½ tsp garlic paste, sautéd in oil

A pinch of salt

Garnish

1 tbsp parsley leaves, chopped

Grind sprouts to a fine paste. Mix the paste with the other ingredients and combine well. Boil the mixture for a few minutes, then reduce the heat and simmer for 15 minutes.

Serve hot, garnished with chopped parsley leaves.

Makes 2 servings

Soya Soup

Nutrition Facts

Calories	26.0 kcal
Carbs	2.6g
Fat	0.1g
Fibre	0.38g
Minerals	0.48g
Protein	3.6g

½ cup soya granules

½ litre water

½ tsp ginger-garlic paste, sautéd in oil

¼ tsp cumin powder

A pinch of salt

Garnish

2 tsp spring onion, chopped

Boil soya granules in water till tender and squeeze out the water. Mix with remaining the ingredients and boil for a few minutes. Reduce heat and simmer for 5-10 minutes.

Serve hot, garnished with chopped spring onion.

Makes 2 servings

Lentil Soup

Nutrition Facts

Calories	183.0kcal
Carbs	29.2g
Fat	3.1g
Fibre	1.7g
Minerals	1.4g
Protein	9.2g

4 tbsp lentils
2 tomatoes, chopped
2 onions small, peeled and chopped
1 tbsp tamarind pulp
½ litre water
¼ tsp pepper powder
¼ tsp cumin powder
¼ tsp coriander powder
½ tsp roasted fenugreek powder
2 tsp curry leaves, roasted
A pinch of asafoetida
A pinch of salt
1 tsp oil

Garnish

2 tsp curry leaves, roasted

Cook the lentils till tender and mash well. Heat the oil and sauté the chopped onions and tomatoes lightly. Add all remaining ingredients, mix well and bring to a boil, then reduce the heat and simmer for 10 minutes.

Serve hot, garnished with the roasted curry leaves.

Makes 2 servings

Tomato & Onion Soup

Nutrition Facts

Calories	104.0 kcal
Carbs	18.7g
Fat	0.61g
Fibre	2.4g
Minerals	2.0g
Protein	5.9g

5 tomatoes, chopped
2 onions, peeled and sliced
½ litre water
¼ tsp pepper powder
1 tsp low fat or skimmed milk powder
A pinch of salt

Garnish

2 tsp mint leaves, chopped

Mix all the ingredients except milk powder, bring to boil and simmer for 15-20 minutes. Liquidize the soup in a mixer while still warm. Dissolve the milk powder in a little water, add to the soup and reheat.

Serve hot, garnished with mint leaves.

Makes 2 servings

Sweetcorn Soup

Nutrition Facts

Calories	69.0 kcal
Carbs	13.4g
Fat	0.49g
Fibre	1.1g
Minerals	0.5g
Protein	2.7g

½ cup corn, ground to a paste
½ litre water
1 tsp ginger, grated
1 green chili
2 flakes garlic, minced
A pinch of salt

Garnish

½ cup corn, boiled
2 tsp mixed herbs, (parsley, mint, basil, coriander leaves) chopped

Boil the water and add all the ingredients. Mix well and simmer for few minutes.

Serve hot, garnished with the mixed herbs.

Makes 2 servings

Cool Cucumber Soup

Nutrition Facts

Calories	90.0 kcal
Carbs	6.5g
Fat	5.1g
Fibre	0.48g
Minerals	1.4g
Protein	4.4g

1 cucumber, large grated
½ litre buttermilk
A pinch of ginger powder
A pinch of salt
Garnish
2 tsp mixed herbs, (parsley, mint, basil, coriander leaves) chopped

Mix all the ingredients to a smooth consistency.

Garnish with the chopped herbs and serve.

Makes 2 servings

Sweet & Sour Chicken Soup

Nutrition Facts

Calories	122.0 kcal
Carbs	8.4g
Fat	2.8g
Fibre	1.6g
Minerals	1.6g
Protein	17.3g

100 g chicken, boiled and shredded
½ litre vegetable stock (see page 90)
1 tbsp soya flour
½ tsp pepper-cumin powder
1 red pepper, chopped
1 tbsp fresh date paste
1 tbsp amla gratings or lime juice
A pinch of salt
Garnish
2 tsp mixed herbs, (parsley, mint, basil, coriander leaves) chopped

Combine the stock and soya flour to a smooth consistency. Add the remaining ingredients except the amla gratings or lime juice and bring to a boil. Simmer for 10-15 minutes. Add the amla gratings or lime juice and mix well.

Serve hot, garnished with the chopped herbs.

Makes 2 servings

Mushroom Salad

Nutrition Facts

Calories	47.0 kcal
Carbs	6.9g
Fat	0.72g
Fibre	0.49g
Minerals	1.0g
Protein	2.3g

100 g button mushrooms
Lime juice dressing (see page 102)
Mixed herb dressing (see page 101)

Garnish

1 tsp mixed herbs, (parsley, mint, basil, coriander leaves) chopped

Clean and boil the mushrooms till just tender and slice horizontally. Place in a serving bowl and spoon over the dressings and toss well.

Garnish with the chopped herbs and serve.

Makes 2 servings

Sweet & Sour Fruit Salad

Nutrition Facts

Calories	87.0 kcal
Carbs	20.0g
Fat	0.44g
Fibre	0.86g
Minerals	0.47g
Protein	0.56g

2 lettuce leaves
1 cup pineapple chunks
1 cup apple diced
1 tbsp honey
Lime juice dressing (see page 102)

Garnish

1 tbsp strawberries, chopped

Mix the pineapple and the apple in a bowl. Mix the dressing and honey and pour over the salad. Toss well. Divide into two portions and place each on a lettuce leaf.

Garnish with the chopped strawberries and serve.

Makes 2 servings

C & C Salad

Nutrition Facts

Calories	53.0kcal
Carbs	9.8g
Fat	0.46g
Fibre	1.1g
Minerals	0.66g
Protein	2.5g

½ cup cauliflower florets
½ cup sweetcorn kernels
Mixed herb dressing (see page 102)
Garnish
2 tsp carrot, grated
2 tsp peas, shelled and parboiled

Boil the cauliflower florets till just tender. Place them with the sweetcorn in a serving bowl. Spoon the herb dressing over and toss well.

Garnish with grated carrot and peas before serving.

Makes 2 servings

Tangy Baby Vegetables Salad

Nutrition Facts

Calories	34.0kcal
Carbs	6.7g
Fat	0.31g
Fibre	0.62g
Minerals	0.48g
Protein	1.1g

2 baby carrots
2 baby radishes
2 baby tomatoes
2 baby corn
Lime juice dressing (see page 102)
Garnish
1 tsp each of grated carrot, grated radish, chopped tomatoes and corn kernels

Place all the vegetables on a serving platter. Spoon the dressing over and toss well.

Garnish with the grated and chopped vegetables and corn kernels and serve.

Makes 2 servings

Citrus Fruit Salad

Nutrition Facts

Calories	69.0 kcal
Carbs	14.5g
Fat	0.36g
Fibre	0.7g
Minerals	0.78g
Protein	1.4g

2 lettuce leaves
2 sweet lime segments
2 orange segments
1 tsp orange or lime peel
Lime juice dressing, (see page 102)
Orange dressing (see page 102)
Garnish
2 tsp mint leaves, chopped

Mix the sweet lime, orange and orange or lime peel in a bowl with the dressings and divide into two equal portions. Place each portion on a lettuce leaf.

Garnish with the chopped mint leaves and serve.

Makes 2 servings

Sweet & Sour Chicken Salad

Nutrition Facts

Calories	110.0 kcal
Carbs	12.6g
Fat	0.57g
Fibre	0.49g
Minerals	0.93g
Protein	13.6g

100 g chicken, boiled and shredded
1 cup mixed citrus fruit segments (orange, sweet lime and grape fruit)
Honey dressing (see page 102)
Garnish
2 tsp mixed herbs, (parsley, mint, basil, coriander leaves) chopped

Mix the salad ingredients and place in a serving dish. Pour the dressing over the salad. Toss well and serve garnished with the chopped herbs.

Makes 2 servings

Curd Dressing

Nutrition Facts	
Calories	25.0 kcal
Carbs	1.7g
Fat	1.4g
Fibre	0.19g
Minerals	0.33g
Protein	1.4g

2 tbsp curd
½ tsp fenugreek powder
A pinch of cumin powder
A pinch of salt

Mix all the ingredients till well combined.

Makes 30 ml serving

Fruity Dressing

Nutrition Facts	
Calories	17.0 kcal
Carbs	3.9g
Fat	0.02g
Fibre	0.2g
Minerals	0.05g
Protein	0.28g

2 tbsp mixed fruit juice
(pineapple, apple orange, etc.)
A pinch of green cardamom powder
A pinch of salt

Mix all the ingredients till well combined.

Makes 30 ml serving

Orange Dressing

Nutrition Facts	
Calories	16.0 kcal
Carbs	3.6g
Fat	0.1g
Fibre	0.15g
Minerals	0.04g
Protein	0.35g

2 tbsp orange juice
A pinch of pepper powder
A pinch of salt

Mix all the ingredients till well combined.

Makes 30 ml serving

Honey Dressing

Nutrition Facts

Calories	16.0 kcal
Carbs	3.6g
Fat	0.1g
Fibre	0.15g
Minerals	0.4g
Protein	0.3g

1 tbsp honey

½ tsp Bishop's weed/dry ginger powder

A pinch of salt

Mix all the ingredients till well combined.

Makes 15 ml serving

Lime Juice Dressing

Nutrition Facts

Calories	15.0 kcal
Carbs	2.7g
Fat	0.27g
Fibre	0.15g
Minerals	0.18g
Protein	0.41g

2 tbsp lime juice

A pinch of salt

A pinch of pepper powder

Mix all ingredients till well combined.

Makes 30 ml serving

More Dressings to Choose From

You can add variety to salad dressings by making slight changes in the choice of ingredients. Here is how you can add different flavours.

Mint	: Use ½ tsp mint leaves paste instead of pepper powder.
Basil	: Use ½ tsp basil leaves paste instead of pepper powder.
Coriander	: Use ½ tsp coriander leaves paste instead of pepper powder.
Mixed herb	: Use ½ tsp mixed herbs paste of mint, coriander, celery and parsley leaves instead of pepper powder.

All variations have approximately the same nutrition value.

Vegetable Delights

About Vegetables & Fruits

- Choose from the several colour options. Include a variety of red, red/purple, orange, orange/yellow, yellow/green and green vegetables and fruits in your diet.
- Nearly all fruits and vegetables are naturally low in fat, replete with filling fibre and loaded with properties that can protect against heart disease and age-related decline in health.
- Fruits and vegetables come closer than any other category of food to the fountain of youth.
- Four to five servings of vegetables, in any form (juices, soups, raitas, salads or as curries), are necessary to maintain fitness.
- Fruits make a healthy snack.

Cluster Beans with Bengal Gram

Nutrition Facts

Calories	183.0kcal
Carbs	34.0g
Fat	6.9g
Fibre	4.6g
Minerals	2.6g
Protein	9.8g

250 g cluster beans, chopped
2 onions, peeled and chopped
½ cup Bengal gram, soaked
1 red chilli, soaked
A pinch of salt
2 tsp oil

Grind the Bengal gram, red chilli and salt to a paste. Steam the paste for 10 minutes. Boil the chopped cluster beans till just tender. Heat the oil and sauté the chopped onions and the steamed paste. Add the cooked cluster beans, stir well and simmer for 2-3 minutes.

Serve with rice or chapatti.

Makes 2 servings

Baby Radish Curry

Nutrition Facts

Calories	139.0kcal
Carbs	14.9g
Fat	5.9g
Fibre	1.0g
Minerals	2.1g
Protein	6.8g

2 baby radishes with greens, chopped
2 onions, peeled and chopped
1 tbsp green gram
1 tsp ginger-garlic paste
A pinch of mustard and cumin seeds
A pinch of salt
2 tsp oil

Heat the oil in a pan and sauté the mustard and cumin seeds and ginger-garlic paste. Add the remaining ingredients with a little water, mix well, cover the pan and cook till the vegetables are tender.

Serve with hot rice or chapatti.

Makes 2 servings

Sautéd Fenugreek

Nutrition Facts

Calories	155.0 kcal
Carbs	14.0g
Fat	4.8g
Fibre	2.5g
Minerals	2.6 g
Protein	8.5g

1 small bunch fenugreek leaves, chopped
1 tbsp green gram
½ tsp curry powder (see page 90)
A pinch of mustard seeds
A pinch of salt
2 tsp oil

Heat the oil in a pan and sauté the mustard seeds. Add the remaining ingredients with a little water to the pan and cook till the contents are tender and dry.

Serve hot with rice or chapatti.

Makes 2 servings

Soya Chunks in Tomato Paste

Nutrition Facts

Calories	174.0 kcal
Carbs	21.6g
Fat	5.6g
Fibre	2.7g
Minerals	2.3g
Protein	9.1g

25 g soya chunks
5 tomatoes
3 onions, peeled
1 piece ginger, about 2-3 cm peeled
4 cloves garlic peeled
A pinch of salt
2 tsp oil

Garnish

2 tsp mixed herbs, (parsley, mint, basil, coriander leaves) chopped

Boil the soya chunks till soft and squeeze out the water. Grind the tomatoes, onions, ginger and garlic to a fine paste. Heat the oil and sauté the paste for few minutes. Add the soya chunks, stir to coat, cover the pan and simmer for 15 minutes.

Garnish with the chopped herbs and serve.

Makes 2 servings

Ambadi Curry

Nutrition Facts

Calories	176.0 kcal
Carbs	24.5g
Fat	6.9g
Fibre	0.47g
Minerals	1.7g
Protein	4.1g

1 small bunch ambadi leaves, chopped
2 onions, peeled and chopped
1 pod garlic, peeled and chopped
A pinch of mustard seeds
A pinch of salt
2 tsp oil
Garnish
1 tsp ginger, grated

Heat the oil and sauté the mustard seeds. Add the chopped onions and garlic and sauté for a minute. Then add the ambadi leaves and salt. Cook, stirring occasionally till done.

Garnish with the grated ginger and serve.

Makes 2 servings

Baked Onions

Nutrition Facts

Calories	108.0 kcal
Carbs	18.8g
Fat	2.8g
Fibre	0.77g
Minerals	0.55g
Protein	1.6g

4 medium sized onions, peeled
2 tbsp lime juice
1 tbsp honey
½ tsp pepper powder
½ tsp cumin powder
¼ tsp fenugreek powder
A pinch of salt
1 tsp oil

Prick the onions with a fork and grease with the oil. Place in a baking dish. Combine the remaining ingredients and pour over the onions. Bake for 15 minutes in a moderately hot oven till tender.

Serve hot with roti or rice.

Makes 2 servings

Sweet-n-Sour Bittergourd

Nutrition Facts

Calories	166.0 kcal
Carbs	23.7g
Fat	5.5g
Fibre	2.6g
Minerals	2.1g
Protein	3.2g

250 g small bittergourds, peeled and sliced
½ cup tomato juice
1 tbsp honey
1 tbsp lime juice
A pinch of pepper
A pinch of cumin powder
A pinch of salt
2 tsp oil

Garnish

2 tsp mixed herbs, (parsley, mint, basil, coriander leaves) chopped

Heat the oil in a pan and sauté the sliced bittergourd for a minute. Add the remaining ingredients, mix well, cover the pan and simmer till the bittergourd is tender.

Garnish with the chopped herbs. Serve hot with rice or chapatti.

Makes 2 servings

Amaranth Curry

Nutrition Facts

Calories	197.0kcal
Carbs	24.8g
Fat	6.2g
Fibre	2.0g
Minerals	6.2 g
Protein	10.6g

1 small bunch amaranth leaves, chopped
2 tbsp green gram or Bengal gram
2 onions, peeled and chopped
1 tsp ginger, grated
5 cloves garlic, peeled and chopped
A pinch of salt

Seasoning

2 tsp oil
1 red chilli, broken into bits
1/4 tsp mustard seeds
1/4 tsp cumin seeds

Cook the amaranth leaves and green or Bengal gram separately till just tender. Heat the oil and sauté the seasoning ingredients, along with the onion, ginger and garlic, for a few minutes. Add the cooked amaranth leaves, the gram and salt to the sautéd mixture and cook for a minute.

Serve with rice or chapatti.

Makes 2 servings

Vegetable Medley

Nutrition Facts

Calories	128.0 kcal
Carbs	15.2g
Fat	5.7g
Fibre	2.6g
Minerals	1.3g
Protein	4.0g

2 each tomatoes, onions, yellow or red peppers, chopped
2 brinjals, diced
2 tbsp peas shelled
2 tsp ginger-garlic paste
A pinch of mustard seeds
A pinch of salt
2 tsp oil
Garnish
2 tsp parsley, chopped

Heat the oil. Sauté the mustard seeds and ginger-garlic paste for a minute. Add the vegetables and salt. Cover the pan. Simmer on low heat till the vegetables are tender.

Garnish and serve hot with rice or chapatti.

Makes 2 servings

Broccoli in Soya Sauce

Nutrition Facts

Calories	118.0 kcal
Carbs	8.6g
Fat	7.3g
Fibre	2.1g
Minerals	1.8g
Protein	8.8g

300 g broccoli florets
½ cup soya sauce (see page 172)
1 tsp ginger-garlic paste
2 tsp oil
Garnish
2 tsp tofu, chopped

Heat the oil in a pan and sauté the ginger-garlic paste for a minute. Add the broccoli and soya sauce. Cover the pan and simmer till the broccoli is tender.

Garnish with chopped tofu. Serve hot with rice or chapatti.

Makes 2 servings

Veggie Bulgur Curry

Nutrition Facts

Calories	307.0kcal
Carbs	55.3g
Fat	6.5g
Fibre	2.7g
Minerals	2.9g
Protein	7.0g

100 g wheat bulgur
2 tsp oatmeal, slightly roasted
1 cup green, red and yellow peppers, cut into strips
1 bunch leeks, chopped
1 green chilli, chopped
4-5 cloves garlic, chopped
1 tsp ginger, grated
3 cups water
A pinch of salt
2 tsp oil

Garnish

2 tsp roasted curry leaves

Roast the bulgur lightly. Heat the oil in a pan and sauté the vegetables for a minute. Add water and salt. Bring to a boil. Add the bulgur and oatmeal, and cook on high flame for 5 minutes. Cover the pan and simmer on low heat till the bulgur is tender.

Garnish with roasted curry leaves. Serve hot with any chutney or curd.

Makes 2 servings

Greeny Rings

Nutrition Facts

Calories	263.0 kcal
Carbs	44.7g
Fat	3.4g
Fibre	2.6g
Minerals	3.2g
Protein	15.5g

100 g whole wheat flour
2 tsp oatmeal
1 tsp fenugreek seeds, roasted and powdered
4 cups mixed green vegetables, chopped
1 tsp ginger garlic paste
1 tbsp gram flour or soya flour paste
2 egg whites (optional)
A pinch of asafoetida
A pinch of salt

Dissolve the salt in water. Mix the other ingredients, except the egg whites (if using), in a vessel till well combined. Add the salt water gradually and knead to a smooth dough. Roll out the dough into 6-inch cylinders and steam for 15 minutes. Slice the steamed cylinders into uniform rings. Brush them with gram flour or egg whites. Preheat oven to a moderate temperature. Place the slices on a greased baking sheet. Bake for 10 minutes.

Serve hot with plain curd or any raita.

Makes 2 servings

Brinjal Bonanza

Nutrition Facts

Calories	108.0kcal
Carbs	12.0g
Fat	5.5g
Fibre	1.8g
Minerals	0.89g
Protein	2.7g

2 brinjals medium sized, diced
2 onions, peeled and chopped
1 tsp ginger-garlic paste
1 tbsp lime juice
A pinch of salt
2 tsp oil
Garnish
½ cup mixed herbs, (parsley, mint, basil, coriander leaves) chopped

Heat the oil and sauté the garlic-ginger paste lightly. Add the brinjal and salt, mix well, cover and simmer till the brinjal is tender. Remove from the heat and add the lime juice.

Garnish and serve with rice or roti.

Makes 2 servings

Steamed Veggie Sensation

Nutrition Facts

Calories	56.0kcal
Carbs	9.3g
Fat	0.66g
Fibre	0.82g
Minerals	0.51g
Protein	3.1g

2 cups mixed vegetables (carrot, potato, peas and green, leafy vegetables), boiled
2 tbsp gram flour
1 tbsp rice flour
1 tbsp soya flour
1 tsp ginger-garlic paste
1 onion, peeled and ground to a paste
A pinch of salt

Make a smooth batter with the flours, onion and ginger-garlic pastes, salt and water. Mash the boiled vegetables and divide into 8 portions. Shape into balls and press lightly. Coat balls with batter and steam for 10 minutes.

Serve with any sauce

Makes 8 servings

Stuffed Tomatoes

Nutrition Facts

Calories	125.0 kcal
Carbs	18.7g
Fat	3.5g
Fibre	1.8g
Minerals	0.9g
Protein	4.7g

4 tomatoes, large firm
½ tsp oil
Filling
4 tbsp peas, shelled and parboiled
4 tbsp tofu, chopped
1 cup rice, cooked
1 tsp ginger-garlic paste
1 onion, ground to a paste
1 tsp mint leaf paste
A pinch of salt
2 tsp oil
Garnish
4 tsp celery leaves, chopped

To prepare the filling combine ginger-garlic paste, onion paste and tofu. Sauté the mixture till light brown. Add the cooked rice, peas, mint leaf paste and salt. Mix well. Divide the filling into four parts.

Slice off the stem end of the tomatoes and scoop out the pulp. Invert them to drain. Lightly grease the tomatoes with oil and bake for few minutes. Cool and gently peel off the skin. Stuff each tomato with one part of the filling and garnish with 1 tsp of chopped celery leaves.

Serve as a mini meal with any raita as an accompaniment.

Makes 4 servings

Stuffed Capsicums

Nutrition Facts

Calories	107.0 kcal
Carbs	15.4g
Fat	3.2g
Fibre	0.7g
Minerals	0.8g
Protein	5.3g

4 capsicums firm
½ tsp oil
Filling
1 cup rice, cooked
2 tbsp soya granules
1 onion, ground to a paste
1 tsp ginger-garlic paste
A pinch of *garam masala* powder
A pinch of salt
2 tsp oil
Garnish
2 tsp parsley leaves, chopped

To prepare the filling, boil the soya granules in water till soft and squeeze out the water. Heat oil and sauté the onion and ginger-garlic pastes for a minute, then add the rice, soya granules, garam masala powder and salt. Divide the filling into four equal parts.

Slice off the stem end of the capsicums and scoop out the seeds. Slightly grease them with oil and bake for few minutes. Stuff each capsicum with one part of the filling. Top the capsicums with chopped parsley.

Serve as a mini meal with any raita as an accompaniment.

Makes 4 servings

Stuffed Onions

Nutrition Facts

Calories	60.0kcal
Carbs	11.1g
Fat	0.8g
Fibre	0.9g
Minerals	0.8g
Protein	2.0g

4 onions, large, peeled
4 tbsp yogurt
A pinch of dry ginger powder
Filling
2 tsp ginger-garlic paste
1 capsicum, chopped
1 pepper, red or yellow, chopped
4 tsp mixed herbs, (parsley, mint, basil, coriander leaves) chopped
A pinch of salt

Halve the onions from the stem to the root. Scoop out the centre and chop. Mix the chopped onions with the ginger-garlic paste, chopped peppers, chopped herbs and salt till well combined.

Divide the filling into eight equal parts. Stuff each onion shell with one part of the filling. Mix the yogurt with the dry ginger powder and apply all over the stuffed onions. Bake in a moderately hot oven till tender. Serve with rice or chapatti.

Makes 4 servings

Pulses & Legumes

About Pulses and Legumes

- Legumes and pulses substitute animal foods in a vegetarian diet.
- Pulses and legumes in combination with cereals improve the quality of proteins in the diet.
- Legumes and pulses with vegetables provide balanced proteins.
- Unsprouted legumes and pulses should always be cooked. Proteins in uncooked pulses (as in chutney powders made from unroasted dal) are not easily digestible.
- Add plenty of herbs like mint coriander, parsley, basil, etc. while cooking legumes and pulses to prevent flatulence and aid digestion.

Soya Sambhar

Nutrition Facts

Calories	147.0kcal
Carbs	18.9g
Fat	3.6g
Fibre	1.9g
Minerals	1.4g
Protein	9.2g

100 g red gram
1 tsp Bengal gram
25 g soya chunks
2 tsp coriander seeds
2 red chillies
1 cup tamarind juice, thin
2 tsp curry leaves
2 tsp corinader leaves
A pinch of asafoetida
A pinch of fenugreek seeds
A pinch of salt

Seasoning

2 tsp oil
A pinch of mustard seeds
A pinch of cumin seeds

Roast the red gram and then pressure cook it till done. Boil the soya chunks and squeeze out the water. Roast the Bengal gram, coriander seeds, fenugreek seeds and red chillies. Powder the mixture. Then mix all the ingredients till well combined. Boil for few minutes or till the mixture is of a smooth consistency. Now the soya sambhar is ready. Heat the oil and sauté the seasoning ingredients. Pour over the soya sambhar.

Serve hot with rice or chapatti.

Makes 4 servings

Sweet & Sour Dal

Nutrition Facts

Calories	251.0 kcal
Carbs	37.1g
Fat	6.0g
Fibre	0.82g
Minerals	1.9g
Protein	12.7g

100 g green gram
2 tbsp lime juice
1 tbsp honey
A pinch of salt
Seasoning
2 tsp oil
½ tsp mustard and cumin seeds
2 red chillies, crumpled
2 tsp curry leaves

Lightly roast the gram, then pressure cook till done. Add the lime juice, honey and salt and mix well. Heat the oil and sauté the seasoning ingredients. Pour over the gram.

Serve hot with rice or chapatti.

Makes 2 servings

Dal with Mustard Greens

Nutrition Facts

Calories	213.0 kcal
Carbs	33.6g
Fat	6.3g
Fibre	1.2g
Minerals	2.7g
Protein	16.8g

100 g lentils
1 bunch mustard greens, chopped
1 tbsp lime juice
A pinch of salt
Seasoning
2 tsp oil
1 green chilli, chopped
A pinch of mustard and cumin seeds

Lightly roast the lentils and cook in water till done. Boil the mustard greens till just tender and drain. Add mustard greens and salt to the cooked dal. Cook for 4-5 minutes, to a smooth consistency. Heat the oil and sauté the seasonings. Pour over the dal.

Serve hot with rice or chapatti.

Makes 2 servings

Methi & Dal Delicacy

Nutrition Facts

Calories	283.0 kcal
Carbs	38.1g
Fat	6.9g
Fibre	2.0g
Minerals	3.6g
Protein	17.3g

100 g green gram

1 medium bunch of fenugreek leaves, chopped

2 tomatoes, chopped

1 green chilli, chopped

½ tsp mustard and cumin seeds

A pinch of salt

2 tsp oil

Lightly roast the green gram. Cook the roasted dal and the vegetables in a pressure cooker till done. Heat the oil and sauté the mustard and cumin seeds. Pour over the dal, add the salt and mix well.

Serve hot with rice or chapatti.

Makes 2 servings

Amaranth Dal

Nutrition Facts

Calories	304.0 kcal
Carbs	39.5g
Fat	8.9g
Fibre	2.3g
Minerals	5.2g
Protein	16.7g

100 g Bengal gram

1 small bunch amaranth leaves, chopped

A pinch of salt

Seasoning

2 tsp oil

1 red chilli, crumpled

½ tsp mustard and cumin seeds

Roast the gram, then pressure cook with the amaranth greens till done. Heat the oil in a pan and saute the seasoning ingredients. Add the cooked dal and salt, mix well. Cook till the dal is of a smooth consistency.

Serve hot with rice or chapatti.

Makes 2 servings

Mixed Sprouted Legumes

Nutrition Facts

Calories	127.0 kcal
Carbs	17.5g
Fat	2.1g
Fibre	1.8g
Minerals	2.1g
Protein	9.5g

100 g mixed legumes, sprouted (whole Bengal gram, soya beans, kidney beans, alfalfa, etc.)

½ cup mixed herb, (parsley, mint, basil, coriander leaves) paste

1 tbsp lime juice

A pinch of salt

Mix lime juice with a pinch of salt. Mix the sprouts and the herb paste in a serving dish. Spoon the lime juice over and toss well.

Serve with any rice preparation or chapatti.

Makes 2 servings

Radish Greens Dal

Nutrition Facts

Calories	294.0 kcal
Carbs	36.8g
Fat	7.1g
Fibre	3.0g
Minerals	3.2g
Protein	17.8g

100 g lentils

1 bunch baby radish with greens, chopped

2 tomatoes, chopped

1 tsp curry powder (see page 90)

A pinch of salt

Seasoning

2 tsp oil

½ tsp mustard and cumin seeds

Roast the gram and cook with the vegetables till done. Heat the oil and sauté the mustard and cumin seeds. Add to the cooked dal, along with the curry powder and salt. Mix well and cook for another minute or till dal is of a smooth consistency.

Serve with rice or chapatti.

Makes 2 servings

Fish & Poultry

About Fish and Poultry

- Fish is a source of high quality protein and essential fatty acids.
- It is rich in B_{12} vitamin, vitamins A and D and minerals.
- Oily fish such as trout, salmon, sardines, fresh tuna, cod, herring, mackerel and halibut are preferable to other varieties. Fish oils are highly protective against heart diseases.
- Buy fresh fish, cook and eat it fresh rather than storing for future consumption.
- Steamed and baked fish is healthier than grilled, smoked, fried or pickled fish.

Lettuce Wrapped Fish

Nutrition Facts

Calories	222.0kcal
arbs	15.7g
Fat	6.0g
Fibre	1.9g
Minerals	3.3g
Protein	26.1g

4 fish fillets
8 lettuce leaves
Marinade
Onion sauce (see page 172)
Soya sauce (see page 172)
Lime juice dressing (see page 102)
2 tsp ginger-garlic paste

Combine the marinade ingredients. Place a piece of fish on two lettuce leaves. Spoon over a quarter of the marinade and gently fold and seal. Repeat with the remaining fish and lettuce leaves. Bake in a moderately hot oven till tender.

Serve with rice or roti.

Makes 2 servings

Fish in Mint-n-Orange Sauce

Nutrition Facts

Calories	133.0kcal
Carbs	6.9g
Fat	2.0g
Fibre	0.18g
Minerals	1.9g
Protein	21.8g

4 fish fillets
For mint-n-orange sauce
100 ml orange juice
1 tbsp lime juice
2 tsp mint leaves paste
1/4 tsp pepper powder
A pinch of salt
Garnish
1 tsp orange peel, grated

Combine the sauce ingredients. Bake or steam the fish. Place the fish in a pan and add the sauce. Mix well, cover and simmer over low heat for 10-15 minutes.

Garnish with the orange peel and serve.

Makes 2 servings

Fenugreek Fish

Nutrition Facts

Calories	137.0 kcal
Carbs	5.0g
Fat	2.6g
Fibre	0.82g
Minerals	2.4g
Protein	23.6g

4 fish fillets
2 cups fenugreek leaves
2 tsp fenugreek seeds, roasted and powdered
1 tbsp lime juice
½ tsp aniseed and cumin powder
A pinch of salt
Garnish
2 tsp tomatoes, chopped

Boil the fenugreek leaves till just tender. Grind to a paste and combine with the remaining ingredients except the fish. Apply the paste evenly to the fish. Wrap each fillet in a banana leaf and steam till tender. Garnish with chopped tomatoes. Serve with rice or roti.

Makes 2 servings

Fish in Garlic Sauce

Nutrition Facts

Calories	174.0 kcal
Carbs	12.4g
Fat	2.9g
Fibre	0.97g
Minerals	2.3g
Protein	24.3g

4 fish fillets
4 tsp garlic paste
¼ tsp pepper and cumin powder
1 tbsp gooseberry paste
1 tsp honey
2 tsp soya flour
A pinch of salt
Garnish: Onion rings and carrot rounds

Steam or bake the fish. Mix all the remaining ingredients with one cup water, bring to a boil and cook till the sauce is thick. Add the fish, cover the pan and simmer for 10 minutes.

Garnish and serve.

Makes 2 servings

Rainbow Chicken

Nutrition Facts

Calories	141.0kcal
Carbs	6.9g
Fat	6.0g
Fibre	1.6g
Minerals	1.7g
Protein	15.0g

100 g chicken, cut into 4 pieces
$^1/_4$ tsp pepper powder
$^1/_4$ tsp cumin powder
1 tbsp lime juice
1 capsicum, chopped
1 red pepper, chopped
1 yellow pepper, chopped
A pinch of salt
2 tsp oil
Garnish
1 spring onion, shredded

Mix salt, pepper, and cumin powder in lime juice and apply the mixture to chicken pieces. Leave for an hour to marinate. Bake in a moderately hot oven till tender. Heat the oil and sauté the chopped peppers and capsicum till they are just tender. Add the chicken, mix well and cook for another minute.
Keep covered till ready to serve.

Garnish with shredded spring onion. Serve hot with rice or chapatti.

Makes 2 servings

Green Garlic Chicken

Nutrition Facts

Calories	87.0 kcal
Carbs	4.5g
Fat	0.62g
Fibre	1.1g
Minerals	1.7g
Protein	15.7g

100 g chicken, cut into 4 pieces
5 cloves garlic, peeled
2 cups mixed herbs (parsley, mint, basil, coriander leaves)
½ cup vegetable stock (see page 90) or plain water
A pinch of salt

Garnish

2 tsp chopped, tomatoes

Bake the chicken in a moderately hot oven till just tender. Meanwhile, grind the garlic and herbs to a smooth paste. Combine the vegetable stock with the garlic and herb paste till it is a smooth mixture and add the salt. Pour this mixture into a pan, add the chicken pieces and simmer over low heat for 20 minutes or till the liquid is reduced to a thick gravy.

Garnish with chopped tomatoes. Serve hot with rice or chapatti.

Makes 2 servings

Red Ginger Chicken

Nutrition Facts

Calories	78.0kcal
Carbs	4.2g
Fat	0.54g
Fibre	0.92g
Minerals	1.2g
Protein	14.0g

100 g chicken, cut into 4 pieces
1 piece ginger, about 6-7 cm
3 tomatoes, large
1 red chilli
½ cup vegetable stock (see page 90)
A pinch of salt
Garnish
2 tsp mixed herbs, (parsley, mint, basil, coriander leaves) chopped

Bake the chicken in a moderately hot oven till just tender. Grind the ginger, tomatoes and red chilli to a smooth paste. Mix the paste and salt with the vegetable stock. Pour the mixture into a pan and add the baked chicken. Simmer on low heat for 20 minutes or till the sauce thickens.

Garnish with the chopped herbs. Serve hot with rice or chapatti.

Makes 2 servings

Chicken Rolls

Nutrition Facts

Calories	87.0 kcal
Carbs	4.5g
Fat	0.62g
Fibre	1.1g
Minerals	1.7g
Protein	15.7g

1 cup whole-wheat flour

A pinch of salt

Filling

100 g chicken, boiled and shredded

1 tsp ginger-garlic paste

2 onions, peeled and chopped

1 cup mixed herbs (parsley, mint, basil, coriander leaves), chopped

½ tsp mixed spice powder (cumin, pepper, Bishop's weed, etc.)

A pinch of salt

2 tsp oil

Dissolve the salt in a little water and add this mixture gradually to the flour. Knead to a smooth dough. Divide the dough into two portions.

Heat 1 tsp oil and sauté the ginger-garlic paste and chopped onions. Add the shredded chicken, chopped herbs, spice powder and a pinch of salt. Mix well and cook for a minute. Divide the filling into two portions.

On a floured board, roll out one portion of dough as thin as possible. Toast it on a hot pan with ½ tsp of oil till both sides are cooked. Spread one portion of the filling evenly over it and roll gently. Repeat with the remaining dough and filling.

Makes 2 servings

Pineapple Curd Chicken

Nutrition Facts

Calories	124.0 kcal
Carbs	9.0g
Fat	2.8g
Fibre	0.89g
Minerals	1.5g
Protein	15.5g

100 g chicken, cut into 4 pieces
1 tsp mixed spice powder (pepper, cumin, Bishop's weed, aniseed, etc.)
1 cup curd
1 cup grated pineapple
A pinch of salt

Garnish

2 tsp herbs, (parsley, mint, basil, coriander leaves) chopped

Mix the spice powder and salt and rub over the chicken pieces. Leave the chicken to marinate for an hour. Then bake in a moderately hot oven till tender. Lightly beat the curd and mix in grated pineapple. Place the cooked chicken in a serving dish, pour the pineapple and curd mixture over it and toss well.

Garnish with the chopped herbs, and serve with hot rice or chapatti.

Makes 2 servings

Orange Chiken with Onion Sauce

Nutrition Facts

Calories	104.0 kcal
arbs	10.9g
Fat	0.45g
Fibre	0.68g
Minerals	1.2g
Protein	13.9g

100 g chicken, cut into 4 pieces
2 large onions, peeled
½ cup vegetable stock
½ cup carrot, grated
½ cup orange segments
A pinch of salt

Garnish

Few mint leaves

To prepare vegetable stock boil vegetables (carrot, tomatoes, cauliflower, cabbage, or any vegetables of your choice) in water with herbs and spices. Cook on a slow fire for 10-15 mintues and strain.

Bake the chicken pieces in a moderately hot oven till just tender. Grind the onions to a smooth paste and mix with the vegetable stock. Add the salt and pour into a pan. Then add the grated carrot and chicken and simmer for 20 minutes till the sauce is thick. Add the orange segments and mix well. Place in a serving dish and garnish with the mint leaves.

Serve with hot rice or chapatti.

Makes 2 servings

Cereals, Rice & Rotis

About Rice, Rotis and Breads

- Rice protein is superior to protein of other cereals.
- Brown rice (unrefined rice) is preferable to refined rice.
- Brown rice is rich in thiamin, niacin, riboflavin, iron, proteins, fat as well as vitamin E and fibre.
- Parboiled rice is more nutritious than refined rice. It is available in most grocery stores.
- White rice is only the starchy endosperm of the kernel, supplying only calories and incomplete protein.

Delicious Rice

Nutrition Facts

Calories	391.0kcal
Carbs	68.9g
Fat	7.3g
Fibre	3.5g
Minerals	2.2 g
Protein	12.1g

100 g rice, cooked
50 g red gram
½ cup tamarind juice, thick
1 cup button onions, peeled
5 cloves garlic, peeled and chopped
1 tsp ginger, grated
1 tsp Bengal gram
2 tsp coriander seeds
2 red chillies
3 cloves
2 cinnamon sticks
3 black cardamoms
3 green cardamoms
A pinch of salt
A pinch of fenugreek seeds
Seasoning
2 tsp oil
2 tsp curry leaves
A pinch of mustard and cumin seeds

Lightly roast the spices and grind them to a powder. Lightly garlic and ginger. Add the cooked red gram, tamarind juice, spice powder and salt, mix well
and cook till nearly all the liquid is absorbed thick. Add the cooked rice and mix well.

Serve hot with raita or plain curd and roasted papad.

Makes 2 servings

Saucy Rice with Mushrooms and Sprouts

Nutrition Facts

Calories	385.0 kcal
Carbs	68.9g
Fat	5.2g
Fibre	3.1g
Minerals	3.5g
Protein	13.8g

100 g rice, cooked
10 button mushrooms, sliced
½ cup kidney beans, sprouted
2 onions, peeled and ground to a paste
2 tsp ginger-garlic paste
Onion sauce (see page 172)
Soya sauce (see page 172)
A pinch of salt
2 tsp oil

Garnish

2 tsp mixed herbs, (parsley, mint, basil, coriander leaves) chopped

Heat the oil in a pan and sauté the ginger-garlic paste for few minutes. Add the sliced mushrooms and sprouted beans and sauté for a minute. Add the sauces, mix well, cover the pan and simmer on low heat for 10 minutes. Add the cooked rice and mix well.

Garnish with the chopped herbs. Serve hot with any raita or plain curd.

Makes 2 servings

Vegetable Khichdi

Nutrition Facts

Calories	257.0 kcal
Carbs	40.9g
Fat	6.0g
Fibre	1.7g
Minerals	1.9g
Protein	9.7g

50 g rice
50 g green gram
2 cups mixed vegetables (broccoli florets, shelled peas, grated carrot, chopped red, green and yellow peppers, and chopped French beans)
¼ tsp pepper powder
¼ tsp cumin powder
A pinch of salt
Seasoning
2 tsp oil
A pinch of mustard seeds
2 tsp curry leaves
Garnish
2 tsp chestnuts

In a pressure cooker, heat the oil and sauté the seasoning ingredients and the vegetables. Add the remaining ingredients and a little over twice the volume of water. Cover the lid and pressure cook.

When done, garnish with chestnuts and serve hot with any chutney or raita.

Makes 2 servings

Herbed Khichdi

Nutrition Facts

Calories	310.0kcal
Carbs	49.5g
Fat	7.0g
Fibre	1.4g
Minerals	2.2g
Protein	11.9g

50 g rice
50 g green gram
1 cup mixed herbs, chopped (coriander, mint, celery, parsley, basil)
1 cup button onions, peeled
1 tsp ginger, grated
1 tsp garlic, chopped
1 tsp oatmeal
2 tsp wheatgerm
1 tsp any bran (wheat, rice or oat)
¼ tsp pepper powder
¼ tsp cumin powder
A pinch of salt

Seasoning

2 tsp oil
A pinch of mustard and cumin seeds
2 tsp curry leaves

Heat the oil in a pressure cooker and sauté the seasoning ingredients, button onions, ginger and garlic for a minute. Add the remaining ingredients and water a little over twice the volume of the rice and pressure cook.

Serve hot with curd or raita.

Makes 2 servings

Chicken Pullao

Nutrition Facts

Calories	310.0kcal
Carbs	49.5g
Fat	7.0g
Fibre	1.4g
Minerals	2.2g
Protein	11.9g

100 g rice, cooked
100 g chicken, cut into 4 pieces
2 onions, peeled
4 cloves garlic, peeled
1 ginger piece, about 2-3 cm
2 tomatoes
1 cup mixed herbs, (parsley, mint, basil, coriander leaves) chopped
A pinch of salt
2 tsp oil
Garnish
Some button onions and cherries, stones removed

Grind the onions, garlic, ginger and tomatoes to a fine paste. Heat the oil in a pan and sauté the paste till light brown. Add the remaining ingredients, mix well, cover the pan and cook till the chicken is tender. Add the cooked rice and stir to mix.

Garnish with the button onions and cherries. Serve with raita and roasted papads.

Makes 2 servings

Roti

Roti is an almost essential part of an Indian meal. In North India roti, and not rice, is the staple food. A finer texture of roti, called *phulka* or chapatti is equally popular. All rotis are made the same way. Only the ingredients may vary, particularly the flour.

Making a Roti: Dissolve the salt in water. Mix all other ingredients in a bowl till they are well combined. Add the water gradually and knead to a smooth dough. Leave aside for 15-20 minutes. Divide the dough into 6 portions on floured board, roll out each ball into rounds of approximately 6 inches. Cook on a heated griddle till both sides are golden and the roti is cooked. Repeat with the remaining dough. Serve hot with any side dish.

Makes 6 servings

You can choose any roti; all are good for the heart.

Methi Roti

Nutrition Facts

Calories	150.0 kcal
Carbs	25.9g
Fat	2.7g
Fibre	2.3g
Minerals	1.3g
Protein	5.7g

200 g wholewheat flour
4 tsp fenugreek seeds, roasted and powdered
¼ tsp pepper powder
¼ tsp cumin powder
2 cups fenugreek leaves, chopped
A pinch of salt

Jowar Roti

Nutrition Facts

Calories	164.0 kcal
Carbs	77.9g
Fat	3.3g
Fibre	0.82g
Minerals	0.72g
Protein	4.2g

200 g jowar flour
2 tsp oatmeal
4 onions, peeled and ground to a paste
2 tsp ginger-garlic paste
A pinch of salt

Garlic Roti

Nutrition Facts	
Calories	148.0kcal
Carbs	25.6g
Fat	3.1g
Fibre	0.7g
Minerals	0.98g
Protein	4.6g

200 g whole wheatflour

1 pod garlic, peeled and ground to paste

A pinch of salt

Ragi Roti

Nutrition Facts	
Calories	161.0kcal
Carbs	26.6g
Fat	3.0g
Fibre	1.4g
Minerals	1.0g
Protein	2.9g

200 g ragi flour

2 onions, peeled and ground to a paste

1 tsp garlic paste

1 tsp ginger paste

1 tsp fenugreek seeds, roasted and powdered

A pinch of salt

Missi Roti

Nutrition Facts	
Calories	161.0kcal
Carbs	26.1g
Fat	3.9g
Fibre	1.6g
Minerals	1.3g
Protein	5.5g

100 g whole wheat flour

100 g whole Bengal gram flour

2 tsp oatmeal

1 bunch spring onion, chopped

1 tsp ginger-garlic paste

A pinch of salt

Bajra Roti

Nutrition Facts

Calories	164.0kcal
Carbs	25.2g
Fat	4.6g
Fibre	0.86g
Minerals	1.5g
Protein	5.6g

200 g pearl millet flour

2 tsp fenugreek seeds

4 cups mixed green leafy vegetables, chopped

1 cup mixed herbs, (parsley, mint, basil, coriander leaves) chopped

A pinch of salt

Dissolve the salt in a little water. Combine all the ingredients. Add water and knead to a smooth dough. Set aside for 15 minutes. Divide the dough into six portions and spread into rounds on a greased plastic sheet. Cook each round on both sides.

Serve hot with any side dish.

Makes 6 servings

Soya Wheat Roti

Nutrition Facts

Calories	193.0kcal
Carbs	23.5g
Fat	6.2g
Fibre	1.3g
Minerals	1.5g
Protein	10.6g

150 g whole wheatflour

1 tsp oatflour

100 g soya beans, boiled

2 onions, peeled

5 cloves garlic, peeled

1 ginger piece, about 2-3 cm

A pinch of salt

Grind the boiled soya beans with onions, garlic and ginger to a fine paste. Dissolve the salt in water. Mix the wheatflour and the paste in a bowl, add water and knead to a smooth dough. Divide the dough into six balls and prepare the rolls *(see page 140)**.*

Serve hot with any side dish.

Makes 6 servings

Raitas

About Curd & Raitas

- Curd is more easily digestible than milk and has all the nutrients of milk.
- The body absorbs twice as much calcium from curd than from milk.
- Include at least one cup of curd in the daily diet.
- Curd protects the stomach from irritation, pain and discomfort and facilitates bowel movement.
- Raitas are combinations of curd and vegetables or fruits.
- Raitas not only provide calcium, protein, vitamins and minerals, but are also a good source of fibre.

Onion Raita

Nutrition Facts

Calories	69.0kcal
Carbs	9.0g
Fat	2.3g
Fibre	0.43g
Minerals	0.85g
Protein	3.2g

1 cup curd

2 onions, peeled and chopped

1 tsp wheatgerm, lightly roasted and boiled

A pinch of salt

Garnish

2 tsp mixed herbs, (parsley, mint, basil, coriander leaves) chopped

Lightly beat the curd to a smooth consistency in a bowl. Add the chopped onions, wheatgerm and salt. Mix well.

Garnish with the chopped herbs. Serve with rice or chapatti.

Makes 2 servings

Herby Raita

Nutrition Facts

Calories	44.0kcal
Carbs	3.5g
Fat	2.2g
Fibre	0.56g
Minerals	0.91g
Protein	2.8g

1 cup curd

2 cups mixed herbs, (parsley, mint, basil, coriander leaves) chopped

A pinch of salt

Garnish

2 tsp grated carrot

Lightly beat the curd to a smooth consistency in a bowl. Add the chopped mixed herbs. Mix well.

Garnish with the grated carrot and serve.

Makes 2 servings

Cucumber & Onion Raita

Nutrition Facts

Calories	74.0 kcal
Carbs	10.5g
Fat	2.2g
Fibre	0.91g
Minerals	1.0g
Protein	2.7g

2 cucumbers medium sized, peeled & grated
2 onions, peeled and chopped
1 cup curd
A pinch of pepper powder
A pinch of salt
Garnish
2 tsp coriander leaves, chopped

Lightly beat the curd to a smooth consistency in a bowl. Add the cucumbers and onions. Mix well. Sprinkle salt and pepper powder over the raita.

Garnish with the chopped coriander leaves. Serve with rice or roti.

Makes 2 servings

Green Vegetable Raita

Nutrition Facts

Calories	56.0 kcal
Carbs	7.5g
Fat	2.7g
Fibre	0.68g
Minerals	1.4g
Protein	2.4g

1 cup curd
2 cups mixed green vegetables, (carrot, peas, cauliflower) chopped
A pinch of pepper powder
A pinch of Bishop's weed powder
A pinch of salt
Garnish
Some cherries, stones removed

Boil the green vegetables till just tender. Add them to the lightly beaten curd along with the remaining ingredients and mix well.

Garnish with the cherries and serve with rice or chapatti.

Makes 2 servings

Mixed Sprouts Raita

Nutrition Facts

Calories	81.0kcal
Carbs	8.7g
Fat	2.9g
Fibre	0.49g
Minerals	0.86g
Protein	5.0g

1 cup curd
1 cup mixed sprouts (whole Bengal gram, soya beans, kidney beans, alfalfa)
A pinch of pepper powder
A pinch of salt

Garnish

2 tsp cherries, chopped

Lightly beat the curd. Add the mixed sprouts, salt and pepper powder. Mix well.

Garnish with the cherries and serve with rice or chapatti.

Makes 2 servings

Pineapple Cooler

Nutrition Facts

Calories	58.0kcal
Carbs	8.0g
Fat	2.1g
Fibre	0.55g
Minerals	0.68g
Protein	2.0g

1 cup curd
1 cup pineapple, grated
2 tsp mixed herbs, (parsley, mint, basil, coriander leaves) chopped
A pinch of salt

Garnish

2 tsp pomegranate seeds

Lightly beat the curd. Add the grated pineapple, mixed herbs and salt to the curd. Mix well.

Garnish with the pomegranate seeds. Serve with rice or chapatti.

Makes 2 servings

Dry Fruit Raita

Nutrition Facts	
Calories	130.0 kcal
Carbs	14.9g
Fat	3.3g
Fibre	1.3g
Minerals	1.5g
Protein	3.0g

1 cup curd

100 g mixed dry fruits (dried figs, apricots, dates and prunes)

Garnish

1 tsp lime peel, grated

Soak the dry fruits overnight and then chop. Add the chopped dry fruits to lightly beaten curd. Mix well.

Garnish with the grated lime peel and serve with rice or chapati.

Makes 2 servings

Crunchy Raita

Nutrition Facts	
Calories	165.0 kcal
Carbs	7.8g
Fat	11.1g
Fibre	0.94g
Minerals	1.5g
Protein	8.7g

2 tbsp watermelon seeds

1 cup curd

1 tbsp Amaranth seeds, roasted

2 tsp mixed herbs, (mint, coriander, celery and parsley leaves) chopped

A pinch of salt

Lightly beat the curd. Add the other ingredients and mix well.

Serve with rice or chapatti.

Makes 2 servings

Desserts

Spicy-n-Crunchy Pears

Nutrition Facts

Calories	149.0kcal
Carbs	23.0g
Fat	5.2g
Fibre	1.2g
Minerals	0.49g
Protein	1.5g

2 pears
2 cloves
2 cinnamon sticks
1 tsp lemon rind
1 cup water
1 tbsp walnuts, chopped
1 tbsp Italian chestnuts, chopped
1 tbsp honey
A pinch of cardamom powder

Peel, core and slice the pears. Place the sliced pears in a pan and add the spices and water. Cook till the pears are tender. Discard the water. Place the pears in a serving dish and allow them to cool. Sprinkle with the chopped walnuts and chestnuts, toss well.

Serve topped with the honey.

Makes 2 servings

Fruity Pudding

Nutrition Facts

Calories	160.0kcal
Carbs	34.7g
Fat	0.29g
Fibre	0.97g
Minerals	1.9g
Protein	4.7g

2 cups skimmed or low fat milk
2 tbsp date paste
2 tbsp black currant paste
2 tbsp raisin paste
A pinch of cardamom powder

Bring the milk to a boil, then reduce the heat and simmer till the quantity of milk is slightly reduced. Add the remaining ingredients. Again simmer on low heat for 8-10 minutes, stirring occasionally.

Cool before serving.

Makes 2 servings

Oatmeal Muffins

Nutrition Facts

Calories	105.0 kcal
Carbs	15.9g
Fat	3.4g
Fibre	0.45g
Minerals	0.44g
Protein	3.1g

60 g wholewheat flour
3 tbsp oatmeal
1 egg white
1 tbsp honey
2 tbsp skimmed milk
1 tbsp oil

Preheat the oven to a moderate temperature. Mix all the ingredients till well combined. Slightly grease six muffin tins with oil. Place equal amounts of mixture in each muffin tin and bake for 15-20 minutes or until done. Cool and store till ready to serve.

Makes 6 servings

Banana Bonanza

Nutrition Facts

Calories	194.0 kcal
Carbs	43.7g
Fat	0.41g
Fibre	0.5g
Minerals	2.7g
Protein	4.1g

2 ripe bananas
1 cup orange juice
1 cup low fat or skimmed milk
A pinch of saffron
A pinch of cardamom powder
Garnish
1 tsp parsley, chopped

Peel the bananas and blend in a mixer with the remaining ingredients to a smooth consistency.

Serve garnished with chopped parsley.

Makes 2 servings

Sweet-n-Savoury Corn Cookies

Nutrition Facts

Calories	62.0kcal
Carbs	10.0g
Fat	1.7g
Fibre	0.48g
Minerals	0.39g
Protein	1.7g

100 g wholewheat flour
2 tbsp oatmeal
½ cup sweetcorn, ground to a paste
¼ tsp pepper powder
¼ tsp cumin powder
1 tbsp honey
½ cup tomato puree
A pinch of salt
1 tbsp oil

To prepare the batter for the cookies, mix all the ingredients to a dropping consistency. Preheat the oven to a moderate temperature. Grease a baking tray with the oil. Spoon the batter in rounds on the baking tray and bake for 15-20 minutes or until the cookies are done. Cool and store.

Makes 12 servings

Carrot Kheer

Nutrition Facts

Calories	94.0kcal
Carbs	21.0g
Fat	0.31g
Fibre	1.4g
Minerals	1.8g
Protein	2.9g

2 carrots, peeled and grated
1 cup skimmed milk, boiled
1 tbsp raisin paste
A pinch of saffron
A pinch of cardamom powder

Pour the milk into a thick bottomed vessel. Add the grated carrots and cook on low heat till the carrots are tender. Add the remaining ingredients and continue to cook on low heat for 10-15 minutes.

Serve hot.

Makes 2 servings

Fresh Fruit Kebabs

Nutrition Facts

Calories	181.0kcal
Carbs	41.3g
Fat	0.84g
Fibre	2.3g
Minerals	0.61g
Protein	1.8g

4 dates, seedless
1 banana, quartered
1 apple, cored and quartered
1 pear, cored and quartered
Marinade
2 tbsp lime juice
2 tbsp tomato puree
1 tbsp honey
½ tsp pepper and cumin powder

Preheat the oven to a moderate temperature.

Prepare the marinade by mixing the marinade ingredients. Smear the fruits with the marinade. Thread the quartered fruits on two skewers and bake for a few minutes.

Serve immediately.

Makes 2 servings

Strawberry Yogurt Dessert

Nutrition Facts

Calories	92.0kcal
Carbs	11.3g
Fat	2.2g
Fibre	1.1g
Minerals	0.8g
Protein	6.6g

2 tsp strawberry flavoured gelatin
1 cup yogurt
10 strawberries, chopped
Garnish
1 tsp mint leaves, chopped

Dissolve the gelatin in half a cup of hot water. When cool, mix with the yogurt and chopped strawberries till well combined and leave to set.

Serve garnished with the chopped mint leaves.

Makes 2 servings

Snacks & Savouries

Idlis

Nutrition Facts	
Calories	97.0 kcal
Carbs	19.3g
Fat	0.53g
Fibre	0.19g
Minerals	0.45g
Protein	3.8g

150 g rice, parboiled
50 g black gram, split
2 tsp oatmeal
2 tsp soya flour
A pinch of salt

Soak the rice and dal in water for 4-5 hours. Grind with enough water to make a thick, smooth batter. Add the remaining ingredients, mix well and set aside to ferment. Pour the batter into idli moulds and steam for 10-15 minutes.

Serve hot with soya sambhar.

Makes 8 servings

Colocassia Slices

Nutrition Facts	
Calories	280.0 kcal
Carbs	40.8g
Fat	7.9g
Fibre	1.6g
Minerals	1.9g
Protein	11.3g

2 large colocassia leaves
4 onions, peeled
1 ginger piece, about 2-3 cm
4 cloves garlic, peeled
2 tomatoes
6 tbsp gram flour
A pinch of mustard seeds
A pinch of salt
2 tsp oil
Garnish
1 tbsp lime juice

Grind onions, ginger, garlic and tomatoes to a fine paste. Add gram flour and salt to the paste and mix well. Apply evenly on colocassia leaves, roll and steam till tender. Slice the rolled leaves, heat the oil and sauté the mustard seeds. Spoon the lime juice over, toss well and serve with chutney.

Makes 2 servings

Green Gram Pancakes

Nutrition Facts

Calories	126.0 kcal
Carbs	19.2g
Fat	2.4g
Fibre	1.3g
Minerals	1.1g
Protein	6.9g

200 g whole green gram, soaked
A pinch of salt
4 tsp oil

Filling

4 onions, peeled and minced
1 cup alfalfa sprouts
2 tsp ginger, grated
3 tsp garlic, chopped
1 cup mixed herbs (parsley, mint, basil, coriander leaves), chopped
1 green chilli, minced
2 tbsp lime juice

Grind soaked green gram and salt to make a smooth batter. Mix all the filling ingredients and divide into eight portions. Pour one ladle of batter in a heated pan and spread as thin as possible. Pour ½ tsp oil over its edges. When the base is cooked, spread one filling portion over it and gently roll the pancake. Repeat till the batter is finished.

Serve hot with raita or plain curd.

Makes 8 servings

Spicy Pancakes

Nutrition Facts

Calories	120.0kcal
Carbs	18.2g
Fat	3.2g
Fibre	0.6g
Minerals	0.69g
Protein	4.4g

100 g wholewheat flour
60 g rice flour
40 g soya flour
3 onions, peeled and minced
1 tsp ginger, grated
2 tsp garlic, minced
2 tsp curry leaves
2 tsp mixed herbs, (parsley, mint, basil, coriander leaves) chopped
A pinch of salt
4 tsp oil

Mix all the ingredients except the oil in a bowl with water to form a smooth batter. Pour one ladle of batter in a heated pan and spread as thin as possible. Pour ½ tsp oil around the edges of the pancakes. When the base is cooked, turn and cook the other side. Repeat till all the batter is used up.

Serve hot with sambhar or chutney.

Makes 8 servings

Khaman Dhokla

Nutrition Facts

Calories	40.0 kcal
Carbs	4.7g
Fat	1.3g
Fibre	0.19g
Minerals	0.32g
Protein	2.3g

160 g gram flour
40 g soya flour
1/2 - 3/4 cup curd
1/2 tsp oil
A pinch of dry ginger powder
A pinch of cumin powder
A pinch of asafoetida
A pinch of salt

Garnish

2 tsp oil
1/2 tsp mustard seeds
2 tsp mixed herbs, (parsley, mint, basil, coriander leaves) chopped

Mix all the ingredients except the oil, till well combined. Set aside for half an hour. Pour the batter into a slightly greased plate, about 6 inches in diameter. Steam for 15 to 20 minutes. Let it cool. Cut into 24 cubes and place on a serving plate. Heat the oil and sauté the mustard seeds. Pour over the dhoklas.

Garnish with the chopped herbs and serve with any sauce.

Makes 4-5 servings

Mixed Legumes Dhokla

Nutrition Facts

Calories	30.0kcal
Carbs	3.3g
Fat	1.0g
Fibre	0.27g
Minerals	0.25g
Protein	1.9g

50 g whole Bengal gram
50 g kidney beans
50 g soya beans
50 g alfalfa
1/2 - 3/4 cup curd
1 tsp ginger-garlic paste
1 onion, peeled and ground to a paste
A pinch of salt
Seasoning
2 tsp oil
1/2 tsp cumin seeds
2 tsp curry leaves

Soak the gram, beans and alfalfa for 4-5 hours, then grind with the salt and curd to a smooth batter. Leave aside for half an hour. Add the ginger-garlic and onion pastes to the batter and pour into a lightly greased plate, about 6 inches in diameter. Steam for 15-20 minutes. Cut into 24 pieces. Heat the oil and sauté the seasoning ingredients. Pour over the dhokla pieces.

Makes 4-5 servings

Plain Dosa

Nutrition Facts	
Calories	123.0kcal
Carbs	20.5g
Fat	3.1g
Fibre	0.21g
Minerals	0.47g
Protein	3.5g

150 g rice
50 g black gram split
2 tsp oatmeal
2 tsp any bran (wheat or rice or oat)
1 tsp wheatgerm, soaked
A pinch of salt
4 tsp oil

Soak the rice and gram together for two hours. Grind with the remaining ingredients with enough water to make a smooth batter. Leave the batter for an hour to ferment. Heat a pan and pour in one ladle of batter and spread as thinly as possible. Pour ½ tsp oil along the edges of the dosa. When the base is cooked, turn and cook the other side.

Serve hot dosas with any chutney or sambhar.

Makes 8 servings

Masala Dosa

Nutrition Facts

Calories	171.0kcal
Carbs	25.8g
Fat	4.4g
Fibre	1.1g
Minerals	1.1g
Protein	7.1g

Dosa batter (see page 162)
4 tsp oil
Filling
2 bunches spring onions, chopped
½ cup soya granules
2 tsp ginger-garlic paste
2 tsp oil
1 tbsp lime juice
A pinch of salt

Boil the soya granules till just tender and squeeze out the water. Heat the oil in a pan and sauté the ginger-garlic paste for a minute. Add the chopped spring onions, mix well, cover the pan and simmer till the spring onions are tender. Add the soya granules along with the salt. Mix well. Stir in the lime juice. Remove from the fire and divide the filling into eight portions.

Pour one ladle of the batter in a heated pan and spread as thin as possible. Pour ½ tsp oil along the sides of the batter. When the base is golden, spread one portion of filling over the top and gently roll the dosa. Repeat till all the batter is used up.

Makes 8 servings

Bhel Special

Nutrition Facts

Calories	190.0 kcal
Carbs	36.8g
Fat	1.2g
Fibre	2.8g
Minerals	2.3g
Protein	6.8g

½ cup sweet corn kernels
½ cup mixed sprouts (alfalfa, kidney beans)
1 cup rice puffs
½ cup wheat puffs (optional)
2 onions, peeled and chopped
2 tomatoes, chopped
1 cup mixed herbs (parsley, mint, basil, coriander leaves) chopped
1 red pepper, chopped
1 yellow pepper, chopped
2 tbsp bhel chutney (see page 169)

Place all the ingredients in a serving bowl. Pour the chutney over and toss well.

Makes 2 servings

Brown Bread Sandwich

Nutrition Facts

Calories	215.0 kal
Carbs	39.4g
Fat	3.5g
Fibre	2.1g
Minerals	1.6g
Protein	6.2g

4 small wholewheat brown bread slices

Filling

4 lettuce leaves
4 each pineapple, onion and tomato slices
4 tsp mint chutney (see page 169)

Slightly toast the bread. Spread 1 tsp of mint chutney on each toast. Place a lettuce leaf on top and over this arrange alternately the pineapple, onion and tomato slices. Cover the filling with another lettuce leaf and top with a second toast. Repeat the process with the rest of the toasted bread and filling.

Makes 2 servings

Bread Upma

Nutrition Facts

Calories	235.0kcal
Carbs	37.7g
Fat	6.3g
Fibre	1.3g
Minerals	0.66g
Protein	6.8g

6 small whole wheat slices of brown bread

2 large onions, peeled and chopped

2 tomatoes, chopped

1 green chilli, chopped

A pinch of salt

Seasoning

2 tsp oil

2 tsp mixed herbs, (parsley, mint, basil, coriander leaves) chopped

A pinch of mustard and cumin seeds

Garnish

2 tsp mixed herbs, chopped

Chop the bread. Heat the oil and sauté the seasoning ingredients. Add the chopped vegetables and sauté for a few minutes. Finally, stir in the chopped bread. Simmer for 5-10 minutes.

Serve hot with any sauce or chutney.

Makes 2 servings

Scrumptious Sandwich

Nutrition Facts

Calories	219.0kcal
Carbs	43.4g
Fat	0.93g
Fibre	2.6g
Minerals	1.9g
Protein	4.3g

4 slices rye bread

2 apple slices

2 pear slices

2 pineapple slices

2 tsp mint chutney (see page 169)

Place a slice each of apple, pear and pineapple between two slices of bread that have been spread with ½ tsp mint chutney. Repeat with the remaining bread.

Makes 2 servings

Peppered Egg Whites

Nutrition Facts

Calories	41.0 kcal
Carbs	2.3g
Fat	0.06g
Fibre	0.24g
Minerals	0.17g
Protein	6.4g

4 egg whites
2 tbsp red pepper chopped
2 tbsp onion, chopped
A pinch of pepper
A pinch of salt
1 tsp oil

Beat egg whites till stiff. Add salt and pepper. Heat and grease a pan. Pour the egg whites into the pan. When one side is set, spread red pepper and onion over the top and fold and cook.

Serve with toast.

Makes 2 servings

Cheezy Eggs

Nutrition Facts

Calories	65.0 kcal
Carbs	2.2g
Fat	2.6g
Fibre	0.28g
Minerals	0.26g
Protein	7.5g

2 eggs, hard boiled
30 g skimmed milk cottage cheese, crumpled
2 tsp onion, finely chopped
4 lettuce leaves
50 g tomato, sliced
A pinch of pepper
A pinch of salt

Cut the boiled eggs vertically into two parts. Remove the yolk. Combine the cottage cheese, onion, salt and pepper. Fill this mixture into the egg whites. Arrange lettuce leaves on a dish and place egg whites on each leaf.

Garnish with tomato slices and serve.

Makes 4 servings

chutneys & sauces

Mint Chutney

Nutrition Facts

Calories	153.0kcal
Carbs	19.9g
Fat	5.8 g
Fibre	2.2g
Minerals	1.7g
Protein	4.7g

½ cup mint leaves
2 tsp tamarind pulp
A pinch of salt
Seasoning
1 tsp oil
1 tsp black gram
1 green chilli
A pinch of mustard seeds
A pinch of fenugreek seeds

Roast the mint leaves lightly. Heat the oil and sauté the mustard and fenugreek seeds and the green chilli. Grind the mint leaves and the sautéd ingredients with the salt to smooth paste.

Makes 4 servings

Bhel Chutney

Nutrition Facts

Calories	88.0kcal
Carbs	18.9g
Fat	0.68g
Fibre	0.57g
Minerals	0.49g
Protein	1.5g

2 tbsp tomato pureé
1 tbsp honey
2 tbsp lime juice
1 tsp oatmeal

Mix all the chutney ingredients till well combined.

Makes 2-3 servings

Garlic Chutney

Nutrition Facts

Calories	45.0 kcal
Carbs	4.3g
Fat	2.6g
Fibre	0.27g
Minerals	0.26g
Protein	1.1g

1 garlic pod, peeled
½ cup coriander leaves
½ cup mint leaves
1 tbsp lime juice
1 green chilli
A pinch of asafoetida
A pinch of salt
2 tsp oil

Heat the oil and sauté the green chilli and garlic lightly. Add other ingredients. When cool grind to a smooth paste.

Serve with hot rice or chapatti.

Makes 4 servings

Onion Chutney

Nutrition Facts

Calories	74.0 kcal
Carbs	11.7g
Fat	2.6g
Fibre	0.83g
Minerals	0.44g
Protein	0.94g

4 onions, peeled and thinly sliced
2 tbsp tamarind pulp
1 tsp honey
1 each red and green chilli
A pinch of asafoetida
A pinch of fenugreek seeds
A pinch of salt
2 tsp oil

Heat 1 tsp oil in a pan and sauté the chilli, asafoetida and fenugreek seeds lightly. Heat the remaining oil in another pan and sauté the sliced onions till just tender. When cool, grind the onions with the other ingredients to a smooth paste

Serve with rice or chapatti.

Makes 4 servings

Ginger Chutney

Nutrition Facts

Calories	39.0kcal
Carbs	2.5g
Fat	2.8g
Fibre	0.7g
Minerals	0.26g
Protein	0.8g

50 g ginger, peeled
1 tbsp lime juice
2 tsp mixed herbs, (parsley, mint, basil, coriander leaves)
A pinch of salt
Seasoning
2 tsp oil
1 each green and red chilli
A pinch of mustard seeds
A pinch of fenugreek seeds
A pinch of asafoetida

Heat the oil and sauté seasoning ingredients. Cool and add the ginger, mixed herbs, lime juice and salt. Grind to make a smooth paste.

Serve with hot rice.

Makes 4 servings

Pickled Beets

Nutrition Facts

Calories	71.0kcal
Carbs	13.7g
Fat	0.51g
Fibre	1.6g
Minerals	1.3g
Protein	2.8g

250 g beetroot, peeled and diced
2 tbsp tomato puree
2 tbsp lime juice
A pinch of pepper powder
A pinch of mustard powder
A pinch of salt

Mix all the ingredients, except the lime juice, in a pan and boil for a minute. Let it cool. Add lime juice and toss well.

Makes 2 servings

Onion Sauce

Nutrition Facts

Calories	151.0 kcal
Carbs	21.4g
Fat	5.7g
Fibre	2.8g
Minerals	1.7g
Protein	3.8g

2 onions, peeled and chopped
4 tomatoes, chopped
½ tsp roasted fenugreek powder
A pinch of pepper powder
A pinch of salt
1 tsp oil

Heat the oil in a pan and add the chopped onions. Sauté for few minutes. Add the remaining ingredients, mix and cover the pan. Cook on a slow fire for 10 minutes. Remove and set aside. While the mixture is still warm liquidize it in the mixer.

Makes 4 servings

Soya Sauce

Nutrition Facts

Calories	54.0 kcal
Carbs	4.0g
Fat	2.1g
Fibre	0.58g
Minerals	0.6g
Protein	4.6g

2 tsp soya flour
½ cup vegetable stock (see page 90)
1 tbsp lime juice
A pinch of pepper powder
A pinch of dry ginger powder
A pinch of salt

Mix all the ingredients and boil for a few minutes. Remove and use as desired.

Makes half cup serving

Thirst Quenchers & Beverages

About Tea and Coffee

- Both tea and coffee contain caffeine.
- Tea is preferable to coffee.
- Limit your intake to a maximum of 2 cups a day.
- Decaffeinated coffee is less harmful than instant or brewed coffee.
- Add only skimmed or low fat milk and little or no sugar to both tea and coffee.

About Fruit and Vegetable Juice

- Liquidized fruit and vegetable juice are excellent health drinks, wholesome and nutritious.
- Never strain fruit or vegetable juice, the fibre which otherwise adds bulk to the diet and is filling will be lost.
- Fibre in fruit and vegetable juice helps bowel movement and prevents constipation.
- Vegetable and fruit juice are full of minerals and vitamins.
- If you dislike eating raw vegetables, the best thing to do is liquidize and drink them as juice.
- Mocktails are better than cocktails.

Ginger Tea/Lemon Grass Tea

Nutrition Facts

Calories	34.0 kcal
Carbs	2.2g
Fat	2.0g
Fibre	0.0g
Minerals	0.4g
Protein	1.6g

1 tsp tea powder
½ tsp ginger, grated
¼ cup low fat or skimmed milk
1 cup water

Boil the water and the grated ginger, then add the tea powder and simmer for a few seconds. Add the decoction to the milk. Stir and serve.

Makes 1 serving

> **Lemon Grass Tea**
>
> Substitute ginger with a few blades of lemon grass and follow the same method as above.

Green Tea

Nutrition Facts

Calories	34.0 kcal
Carbs	2.2g
Fat	2.0g
Fibre	0.0g
Minerals	0.4g
Protein	1.6g

½ tsp green tea
¼ cup milk
1 cup water

Boil the water, stir in the tea and simmer for a minute, add the milk then remove from the fire, and serve.

Makes 1 serving

Mango Mania

Nutrition Facts

Calories	156.0 kcal
Carbs	24.8g
Fat	4.5g
Fibre	1.2g
Minerals	1.4g
Protein	4.0g

1 cup mango pulp
200 ml (1 medium sized glass) buttermilk
A pinch of green cardamom powder
A pinch of dry ginger powder
Garnish
3-4 mango cubes
½ tsp basil leaves, chopped

Liquidize the ingredients in blender and pour the mixture into a tall glass.

Garnish with the mango cubes and chopped basil leaves.

Makes 1 serving

Tomato Twister

Nutrition Facts

Calories	87.0 kcal
Carbs	18.6g
Fat	0.47g
Fibre	2.2g
Minerals	1.7g
Protein	1.9g

2 tomatoes
1 carrot, peeled
1 tsp honey
200 ml water
A pinch of pepper powder
Garnish
1 tsp roasted curry leaves

Liquidize the tomatoes and carrot in a blender and mix with the water. Add the honey and pepper powder and mix well.

Serve garnished with roasted curry leaves.

Makes 1 serving

Green All rounder

Nutrition Facts

Calories	53.0kcal
Carbs	8.9g
Fat	0.64g
Fibre	1.3g
Minerals	1.1g
Protein	2.8g

1 cup mixed herbs (parsley, mint, basil, coriander leaves)
1 tsp honey
1 tsp lime juice
A pinch of Bishop's weed powder
Garnish
½ tsp grated lime peel

Grind the herbs to a fine paste. Add the paste and the remaining ingredients to a glass of water. Blend and pour into a tall glass.

Garnish with grated lime peel and serve.

Makes 1 serving

Mint Lemonade

Nutrition Facts

Calories	36.0kcal
Carbs	7.4g
Fat	0.28g
Fibre	0.2g
Minerals	0.39 g
Protein	0.84g

2 tbsp lime juice
2 tbsp mint leaves
1 tsp honey
200 ml water
Garnish
½ tsp grated lime peel

Grind the mint leaves to a paste and blend with the water and other ingredients in a mixer. Pour into a tall glass.

Garnish with the grated lime peel and serve.

Makes 1 serving

Citrus Temptation

Nutrition Facts

Calories	82.0 kcal
Carbs	18.5g
Fat	0.27g
Fibre	0.2g
Minerals	0.22g
Protein	1.6g

75 ml orange juice
75 ml sweet lime juice
1 tbsp lime juice
A pinch of cumin powder
Garnish
½ tsp orange peel, grated
½ tsp lime peel, grated

Blend all the ingredients in a blender. Pour the mixture into a tall glass.

Serve garnished with the grated orange and lime peel.

Makes 1 serving

Pineapple Punch

Nutrition Facts

Calories	123.0 kcal
Carbs	28.4g
Fat	0.42g
Fibre	1.7g
Minerals	1.1g
Protein	1.4g

4 slices pineapple
3 cherries, stones removed
2 strawberries
200 ml water
A pinch of pepper powder
Garnish
1 tsp parsley leaves, chopped

Liquidize the ingredients in a blender and pour the mixture into a glass.

Garnish with the chopped parsley and serve.

Makes 1 serving

Papaya Passion

Nutrition Facts

Calories	68.0kcal
Carbs	14.7g
Fat	0.42g
Fibre	1.9g
Minerals	1.1g
Protein	1.4g

Few slices of papaya, deseeded
200 ml water
A pinch of Bishop's weed powder

Garnish

1 tsp celery leaves, chopped

Liquidize the papaya with the water and Bishop's weed and pour into a tall glass.

Serve garnished with the chopped celery leaves.

Makes 1 serving

Merry Mocktail

Nutrition Facts

Calories	118.0kcal
Carbs	26.3g
Fat	1.1g
Fibre	4.6g
Minerals	1.4g
Protein	1.7g

1 cup mixed fruits (apple, peach, orange, grapes)
200 ml water
A pinch of aniseed powder
A pinch of cumin powder

Garnish

½ tsp orange peel, grated
1 tsp pomegranate seeds

Combine all the ingredients in a blender and pour into a tall glass.

Garnish with the grated orange peel and pomegranate seeds. Serve.

Makes 1 serving

Pina Carrot Punch

Nutrition Facts

Calories	102.0 kcal
Carbs	22.7g
Fat	0.44g
Fibre	2.1g
Minerals	1.7g
Protein	1.7g

2-3 slices pineapple
1 carrot, peeled
200 ml water
A pinch of pepper powder
Garnish
1 tsp mixed herbs, (mint, coriander, celery and parsley leaves) chopped

Liquidize all the ingredients with the water in a blender and pour into a tall glass.

Serve garnished with the chopped mixed herbs.

Makes 1 serving

Fruity Milk

Nutrition Facts

Calories	70.0 kcal
Carbs	12.9g
Fat	0.3g
Fibre	0.38g
Minerals	1.2g
Protein	3.9g

2 cups skimmed milk or low fat milk
1 cup mixed fruits (apple, pineapple, and any seasonal fruit except citrus fruit), chopped

Boil and cool the milk. Pour into two bowls. Spoon half the chopped fruits into each bowl.

Stir and serve immediately.

Makes 2 servings

Soya Shake Malt

Nutrition Facts

Calories	131.0kcal
Carbs	16.0g
Fat	5.6g
Fibre	0.05g
Minerals	0.26g
Protein	5.3g

200 ml soya milk
1 tbsp alfalfa sprouts, fresh or dried, powdered
1 tsp raisins
A pinch of cardamom powder
Garnish
Few basil leaves

Blend all the ingredients till smooth and foamy. Pour the mixture into a tall glass.

Serve garnished with a few basil leaves.

Makes 1 serving

Soya Mocktail

Nutrition Facts

Calories	184.0kcal
Carbs	28.2g
Fat	3.3g
Fibre	1.1g
Minerals	1.8g
Protein	10.7g

200 ml coconut water or plain water
4 tsp soya flour
20-25 red grapes
1 orange segments
1 pineapple slice
A pinch of cardamom powder
Garnish
Some cherries and mint leaves

Blend all the ingredients in a blender till smooth and foamy. Pour into a tall glass.

Serve garnished with the cherries and mint leaves.

Makes 1 serving

Strawberry Surprise

Nutrition Facts

Calories	122.0 kcal
Carbs	13.7g
Fat	5.4g
Fibre	1.1g
Minerals	1.4g
Protein	4.7g

5 strawberries
1 glass buttermilk
Garnish
1 scoop thick yogurt
1 tsp chopped strawberries

Liquidize the ingredients in a blender till frothy. Pour into a tall glass and top with the yogurt. Sprinkle the chopped strawberries on top.

Makes 1 serving

Apple Gingerale

Nutrition Facts

Calories	77.0 kcal
Carbs	17.6g
Fat	0.52g
Fibre	1.1g
Minerals	0.34g
Protein	0.28g

1 apple, cored and chopped
2 tsp ginger juice or a pinch of dry ginger powder
1 tsp honey
200 ml water
Garnish
1 scoop thick yogurt
½ tsp grated ginger

Liquidize all the ingredients with the water in a blender. Serve with a pinch of grated ginger.

Makes 1 serving

Appendices

Cooking Terms

Bake	:	To cook food by dry heat, usually in an oven.
Blend	:	To combine ingredients in a mixer.
Boil	:	To heat the mixture or a liquid until bubbles appear on the surface and vapour starts rising.
Batter	:	A thick mixture of flour and liquid, i.e. water, milk, etc.
Blanch	:	To remove peel or skin from food after soaking in boiling water for about a minute.
Drain	:	To strain the liquid from a food leaving it dry or drier.
Deseed	:	To remove the seed.
Dough	:	To mix flour and liquid till the dough is thick enough to knead, but too stiff to stir or pour.
Garnish	:	To decorate food.
Grate	:	To rub food to shred into small pieces on a grater.
Grind	:	To reduce food to a paste.
Gravy	:	Liquid in which the food is cooked.
Knead	:	To work dough with hand pressing, stretching and folding until it reaches a desired consistency.
Parboil	:	To cook partly by boiling.
Roll	:	To place a ball of dough on a flat surface and spread with a rolling pin.
Sieve/ Sift	:	To separate coarse pieces from the fine by shaking through a sieve.
Simmer	:	To cook over low heat just below boiling point.
Steam	:	To cook by contact with live steam in a container placed over hot water.
Stir	:	To mix ingredients together within a container, usually by means of a spoon.
Sauté	:	To brown food lightly over medium heat in very little fat, preferably polyunsaturated fatty acid (PUFA).
Shred	:	To cut food into small, long and narrow pieces.
Toast	:	To cook food in a pan with a little fat till crisp.

7-day Sample Menus for the Heart Patients*

Day 1

Bed Tea

Tea 1 cup** + 2 Marie Biscuits

Breakfast

Milk/Milk Pudding	1 cup
Vegetable *Paratha* with mint chutney	1
Chikoo	1

Midmorning

Buttermilk	1 glass**

Lunch

Soup, Cold cucumber	1 cup
Jowar *Roti*	2
Lentils	1 cup
Amaranth curry	1 cup
Stuffed tomatoes	1 cup
Onion raita	1 cup
Baked apple surprise	1 cup

4.00 p.m.

Skimmed milk	1 cup
Brown bread sandwich	1 cup
Apple, medium	1

6.00 p.m.

Orange juice	1 glass

Dinner

Phulka (Chapatti)	2
Mixed sprouted legumes	1 cup
Broccoli in soya sauce	1 cup
Curd	1 cup

Bed Time

Milk	1 cup

Day 2

Bed Tea

Tea 1 cup + 2 Marie Biscuits

Breakfast

Milk/Milk Pudding	1 cup
Poha (rice flakes)	1 cup
Orange	1

Midmorning

Sweet lime juice	1 glass

Lunch

Sprouty soup	1 cup
Ragi *roti*	2
Moth beans curry	1 cup
Mixed vegetables curry	1 cup
Fenugreek curry	1 cup
Tomato raita	1 cup
Melony bowls	1 cup

4.00 p.m.

Skimmed milk	1 cup
Bhel (without *sev*)	1 cup
Peach, medium	1

6.00 p.m.

Amla juice	1 glass

Dinner

Phulka (Chapatti)	2
Plain dal	1 cup
Cabbage onion curry	1 cup
Curd	1 cup

Bed Time

Milk	1 cup

* Diet restricted to 1500 kcal/day. Use of salt restricted to cooking only.
** 1 cup is 150 ml, 1 glass is 250 ml.

Day 3

Bed Tea

Tea 1 cup + 2 Marie Biscuits

Breakfast

Milk/Milk Pudding	1 cup
Dhokla with coriander chutney	2-3 pcs.
Sweet lime	1 cup

Midmorning

Pink grapes juice	1 glass

Lunch

Phulka (Chapatti)	2
Lentil soup	1 cup
Herby Raita	1 cup
Baby salad	1 cup
Brinjal curry	1 cup
Fruity yogurt	1 cup

4.00 p.m.

Skimmed milk	1 cup
Khaman dhokla	2-3 pcs.
Strawberries	3-4

6.00 p.m.

Water melon juice	1 glass

Dinner

Greeny rings	1 cup
Mung dal *khichdi*	1 cup
Veggie variety	1 cup
Curd	1 cup

Bed Time

Milk	1 cup

Day 4

Bed Tea

Tea 1 cup + 2 Marie Biscuits

Breakfast

Milk	1 cup
Idlis with soya *sambhar*	2
Banana, medium	1

Midmorning

Tomato juice	1 glass

Lunch

Wholesome vegetable soup	1 cup
Rice	1 cup
Mustard greens dal	1 cup
Sweet-n-sour Bittergourd curry	1 cup
Curds	1 cup
Fresh fruit kebabs	1 cup

4.00 p.m.

Skimmed milk	1 cup
Plain *dosa*, medium	2
Plums	3-4

6.00 p.m.

Barley water/fruit juice	1 glass

Dinner

Rice	1 cup
Mixed legumes delicacy	1 cup
Tender radish curry	1 cup
Curd	1 cup

Bed Time

Milk	1 cup

Day 5

Bed Tea

Tea 1 cup + 2 Marie Biscuits

Breakfast

Milk with wheat flakes & chopped mixed fruits	1 cup

Midmorning

Carrot juice	1 glass

Lunch

Sweet corn soup	1 cup
Brown bread slices	2
Sweet-n-sour fruit salad	1 cup
Tender radish curry	1 cup
Baked vegetables	1 cup
Strawberry yogurt	1 cup

4.00 p.m.

Soya milk or lassi	1 cup
Colocassia slices	1 cup

6.00 p.m.

Mixture of coconut water and fruit juice	1 glass

Dinner

Toasted brown bread	2
Boiled rice	1 cup
Sprout stuffed capsicums	1
Mixed vegetable raita	1 cup

Bed Time

Milk	1 cup

Day 6

Bed Tea

Tea 1 cup + 2 Marie Biscuits

Breakfast

Curd	1 cup
Roti	1
Pear	1 cup

Midmorning

Mixture of soya milk and fruit juice	1 glass

Lunch

Tomato onion soup	1 cup
Missi roti	2
Soya chunks curry	1 cup
Ambadi curry	1 cup
Vegetable salads	1 cup
Curds	1 cup
Fruit salad	1 cup

4.00 p.m.

Milk	1 cup
Bread *upma*	1 cup
Pink grapes	1 cup

6.00 p.m.

Strawberry juice	1 glass

Dinner

Veggie *khichdi*	1 cup
Dal	1 cup
Mixed vegetable raita	1 cup
Curd	1 cup

Bed Time

Milk	1 cup

Day 7

Bed Tea

Tea 1 cup + 2 Marie Biscuits

Breakfast

Milk/milk pudding	1 cup
Veggie bulgur	1 cup
Guava	1

Midmorning

Citrus juice	1 glass

Lunch

Soya soup	1 cup
Phulka (Chapatti)	2
Clustered beans curry	1 cup
Spring onion curry	1 cup
Crunchy pear	1

4.00 p.m.

Milk or *lassi*	1 cup
Brown bread sandwich	1
Papaya slices	2-3

6.00 p.m.

Mixed vegetable juice	1 cup

Dinner

Mixed vegetable stuffed *dosa* or pancake	1
Mixed boiled legumes	1 cup
Curds	1 cup

Bed Time

Milk	1 cup

Sample menu for heart patients working in a sedantry job

- Special rice
- Chapatti, herby-healthy ***khichdi*** or bhakri-bhaji
- Mixed vegetable-sprouts biryani or pullao
- Saucy rice with mushrooms and sprouts
- Rice with mixed vegetable dal poured over it
- Mixed dal-rice pancake with a gravy vegetable curry
- Vegetable-low fat cheese slices brown bread sandwich
- Vegetable ***khichdi***

Glossary of Cooking Ingredients

Cereal Grains and Products

Barley, *Jau*
Jowar, *Jaur*
Maize, *Makka*
Oat meal, *Jav*
Pearl millet, *Bajra*
Ragi (finger millet), *Madua*
Rice (parboiled), *Usnachawal*
Rice bran, *Konda*
Rice flakes, *Chewra*
Rice, puffed, *Murrmura*
Sago, *Sabudana*
Semolina, *Sooji*
Vermicelli, *Sewain*
Wheat flour, refined, *Maida*
Wheat, bulgar, *Lapsi*
Wheat flour, whole, *Gehun ka atta*

Pulses and Legumes

Bengal gram, roasted, *Bhuna chana*
Bengal gram, split, Chane-ki-dal
Bengal gram, whole, *Kabuli chana*
Black gram, split, *Urad dal*
Field beans, *Sem*
French beans, *Rajmah*
Green gram, whole, *Mung*
Green gream, split, *Mung dal*
Horse gram, *Kulthi*
Kidney bean, *Moth*
Lentil, *Masur dal*
Moth beans, *Moth*
Red gram, *Arhar (tuvar) dal*

Leafy Vegetables

Amaranth, *Chauli saag*
Brussels sprouts, *Chotee gobee*
Celery leaves, *Ajwain-ka-patta*
Colocasia leaves, *Arvi-ka-saag*
Coriander leaves, *Hara dhania*
Curry leaves, *Kadipatta*
Fenugreek leaves, *Methi saag*
Lettuce, *Salad ka patta*
Mint, *Pudina*
Mustard leaves, *Sarson-ka-saag*
Radish leaves, *Mooli saag*
Red spinach, *Poi (mayalu)*
Spinach, *Palak*
Turnip greens, *Shalgam-ka-saag*

Root Vegetables

Beetroot, *Chukandar*
Colocasia, *Arvi*
Radish, *Mooli*
Turnip, *Shalgam*

Other Vegetables

Asparagus, *Shatwar, Sootmooli*
Bitter gourd, *Karela*
Capsicum, *Simla mirch*
Cluster beans, *Guar-ki-phalli*
Cucumber, *Khira*
Drumstick, *Saijan-ki-phalli*
Field beans, *Kulthi*
French beans, *Bhakla*
Knol-khol, *Kohl-rabi*
Leeks, *Vilayiti pyaz*
Mushrooms, *Tila chhattoo*
Ridge gourd, *Torai*
Round gourd, *Tinda*
Spring onion, *Hara pyaz*

Nuts, Oil Seeds, Seeds and Oils

Amaranthus, seeds, *Rajkheera*
Groundnut oil, *Mungaphali ka tel*
Mustard oil, *Rai ka tel*
Mustard seeds, *Rai*
Safflower oil, *Kardi tel*
Sesame oil, *Til ka tel*
Sunflower oil, *Surya mukhi tel*
Walnut, *Akhrot*
Water chestnut, *Shingara*
Water melon, seeds, *Tarbuj ka beej*

Condiments and Spices

Asafoetida, *Hing*
Cardamum, black, *Kala elaichi*
Cardamum, green, *Hara elaichi*
Cloves, *Laung*
Coriander seeds, *Dhania*
Cumin seeds, *Jira*
Fenugreek seeds, *Methi*
Garlic, *Lassoon*
Ginger, *Adrak*
Lime peel, *Nimbu ka chhilka*
Nutmeg, *Jaiphal*
Omum/Bishop's, seeds, *Ajwain*
Pepper, *Kali mirch*
Poppy seeds, *Postdana*
Tamarind, *Imli*
Turmeric, *Haldi*

Fruits

Apricot, *Khoomani*
Black plum, *Jamun*
Cherries, *Gilas*
Currants, black, *Munakka*
Custard apple, *Sharifa*
Dates, *Khajur*
Figs, *Anjeer*
Indian gooseberry, *Amla*
Indian plum, *Ber*
Lemon, sweet, *Mitha neembu*
Lime, *Neembu*
Lime, sweet, *Musambi*
Melon, musk, *Kharbooja*
Melon, water, *Tarbuj*
Mulberry, *Shahtoot*
Papaya, *Papita*
Peaches, *Aarhoo*
Pears, *Nashpati*
Pineapple, *Ananas*
Plum (dried plums are prunes), *Alubokhara*
Pomegranate, *Anar*
Raisins, *Kishmish*
Raspberry, *Rusbhary*
Sapota, *Sapota or Chikoo*
Strawberry, *Istabari*
Woodapple, *Kaith*

	Calcium	Fibre	Folic	Iron	Lecithin	Magnesium	Potassium	Selenium	B-carotene	Vitamin B	Vitamin C	Vitamin E	Vitamin K
Apricots		•		•				•		•			
Apples		•				•					•		
Alfalfa						•		•					
Artichokes				•					•				
Asparagus				•					•		•	•	
Bananas		•					•				•		
Beet Roots				•	•			•				•	
Bean Sprouts				•							•	•	•
Black Currants									•				•
Broccoli				•	•				•		•		•
Brussels Sprouts		•	•							•		•	
Buttermilk	•								•				
Cabbage		•	•					•			•	•	•
Cauliflower									•				•
Carrots		•								•			
Citrus Fruits		•	•			•	•				•		
Cucumber				•							•		•
Custard Apple									•				•
Curd	•								•				
Dates					•		•	•				•	
Dried Beans		•	•	•			•						•
Fruits		•								•	•	•	•
Figs	•				•		•	•					
Fruit Juices				•						•	•	•	•
Guavas		•						•				•	
Gooseberries													•
Green Leafy Veg.	•			•	•			•	•	•	•	•	
Green Peas		•	•									•	

Which are Beneficial to Heart

	Calcium	Fibre	Folic	Iron	Lecithin	Magnesium	Potassium	Selenium	B-carotene	Vitamin B	Vitamin C	Vitamin E	Vitamin K
Knolkhol		•						•				•	
Kiwi Fruit		•						•		•		•	
Leeks				•					•				
Mango											•		•
Milk & Milk Products	•								•			•	•
Mushrooms				•					•				
Nuts	•				•				•			•	•
Papaya											•		•
Pears	•		•		•				•				•
Peaches								•					•
Peppers											•		•
Pineapple													•
Pomegranate													•
Potatoes			•						•				•
Plums									•			•	•
Prunes			•	•					•				
Pumpkin Seeds					•			•	•				
Raisin					•				•				
Raspberries			•	•									•
Soyabeans			•	•	•	•		•	•				
Sweet Potatoes									•		•		•
Strawberry									•				•
Tomatoes									•			•	•
Tofu	•				•								•
Vegetables			•							•	•	•	•
Whole Grain Cereals			•		•	•		•	•				•